digital
photo illustration

Jeremy Gardiner

digital photo illustration

VAN NOSTRAND REINHOLD
NEW YORK

Library of Congress Catalog Card Number 93-21057
ISBN 0-442-01167-9

I(T)P   Van Nostrand Reinhold is an International Thomson Publishing company.
ITP logo is a trademark under license.

Design and typography by Patrick Seymour
Printed in the Hong Kong

Van Nostrand Reinhold
115 Fifth Avenue
New York, NY 10003

International Thomson Publishing GmbH
Konigswinterer Str. 518
5300 Bonn 3
Germany

International Thomson Publishing
Berkshire House,168-173
High Holborn, London WC1V 7AA
England

International Thomson Publishing Asia
38 Kim Tian Rd., #0105
Kim Tian Plaza
Singapore 0316

Thomas Nelson Australia
102 Dodds Street
South Melbourne 3205
Victoria, Australia

International Thomson Publishing Japan
Kyowa Building, 3F
2-2-1 Hirakawacho
Chiyada-Ku, Tokyo 102
Japan

Nelson Canada
1120 Birchmount Road
Scarborough, Ontario
M1K 5G4, Canada

CP 16 15 14 13 12 11 10 9 8 7 6 5 4 3 2 1

Gardiner, Jeremy
    Digital photo illustration/Jeremy Gardiner.
        p. cm.
    Includes bibliographical references and index.
    ISBN 0-442-01167-9
    1. Photography—Digital techniques. 2. Computer graphics—Equipment and supplies.
I. Title.
TR267.G37   1994
771—dc20

93-21057
CIP

Dedicated to the memory of Jim Pomeroy

Contents

Contributors' Affiliations

Martha Rosler is an artist and writer specializing in issues of representation and of urbanism. She is Graduate Director and a professor in the Art Department of Rutgers University.

Murray Oles is Corporate Vice President of Applied Graphics Technologies. Prior to this appointment he was manager of Applied Graphics Super Studio in New York City, where he was in charge of workflow and equipment purchases.

Pat Johnson is a contributing editor to numerous technical computer graphics publications including Advanced Imaging and Photo Electronic Imaging. She is currently a professor of Computer Graphics at Pratt Institute and Miami Dade Community College. She conducts product research for Polaroid, Iris, and other electronic imaging manufacturers.

Jim Kilkelly has spent twenty years in all phases of commercial photography. Since 1985 he has focused on digital imaging techniques, consulting for manufacturers and small business and contributing to industry publications such as *Photo District News* and *Advanced Imaging*. He teaches at the Center for Creative Imaging in Camden, Maine, and at the School of Visual Arts.

J. Nevin Shaffer, Jr. is a partner of Shaffer and Culbertson in Austin, Texas, an intellectual property law firm specializing in patent, trademarks, copyright, trade secrets, and unfair competition law. He is currently president of the Austin Intellectual Property Law Association.

Preface

Digital Photo Illustration is written for everyone, everywhere, who needs to master the fast-changing techniques and technologies now revolutionizing the graphic arts. Illustrators, artists, photographers, retouchers, art directors, ad agencies, printers, prepress shops, publishers, art students, educators, and others who all need practical, reliable guidance about the way digital images are designed, stored, corrected, and manipulated for print. We must all decide whether we want to walk through the door that technology provides. If we do, this book is the key. There are numerous books about the subject of computer graphics, its history and techniques, and the people, the programs, and the machines that make the images that are becoming the visual currency of our lives. But until now there has not been one exclusively devoted to digital photo illustration.

So this book is unique. Each chapter has a discussion of the technical and nontechnical barriers facing artists and designers today. For too long, digital photo illustration has been judged on the quality of the tools used to create it, not the quality of the idea behind it. Technology alone is not enough to ensure the quality of an idea, and we cannot return to a pre-technological existence, so we must begin a dialogue with the computer while being fully aware of its nonneutrality.

Through first-hand experience and observation, the author has determined what methods best serve a particular project. This book is a guide that attempts to introduce the fundamental concepts of creative design for color electronic prepress and lay a foundation that can be used as the basis for further work in the field. The two primary areas of image synthesis are electronic photo assembly and digital illustration techniques. Conceptually these are different problems but, practically, there is much overlap. Various decisions made in the design of a montage will usually have an impact on other areas. This material is written to be accessible to anyone who has a basic knowledge of two-dimensional paint systems and wishes a more advanced background in image synthesis techniques.

As artists are increasingly utilizing the opportunities to function in a world that is increasingly relying on digital technology to get their messages across, new styles will be forged to define the epoch and its ideas. However, it is important at this point not to confuse scientific advancement in computer graphics with artistic advancement. The meaning of pictorial representation develops in a nonlinear fashion — unlike computer science, which has a logical progression. Computers are easy to use and they have begun to stimulate creativity, but while the technology enhances talent, it is no substitute for it. I hope this book will act as a catalyst dissolving media boundaries and awakening newcomers to the possibilities of digital photo illustration.

Many friends and colleagues have been very kind and helpful in the preparation of this book. I wish to acknowledge Professor Isaac Kerlow, Chairman of Computer Graphics at Pratt Institute of Art and Design in New York, for his courtesy and willingness to let me take a leave of absence to work on this project. I am most appreciative of the chapters by all the contributors who generously agreed to write on their areas of speciality. I should like to thank all of the artists represented in this book, all of whom worked very closely with me to create images spanning all aspects of digital photo illustration. These images will be a yardstick by which all digital photo illustration will be judged in the future.

I am most appreciative of the insights and comments of my editors, Amanda Miller and Wendy Lochner. I was fortunate to have three dedicated assistants in Brenda Garcia, Yvonne Channel, and Deborah Hasselmark. Many thanks are also due to Olga Spiegel and Mary Lowenbach, who did much of the photography for the book.

I should also like to thank all the specialists for their professional direction, beginning with Brad Dorin and Michael Kanfer at Printbox in New York. Also Craig Jordan and John Knepper at Imagebank in New York for their continuing support and generous loan of Imagebank's own copyrighted stock photography for many of the projects. I am deeply grateful to Baldev and David Duggal of Duggal Color Projects for their contribution of images. I would also like to extend my thanks to David Throup and Roger Thornton at Quantel in Newbury, England, Peter Brehm at the Graphic Communication Association in Arlington, Virginia, and Eugene Hunt at the Agfa Compugraphic Division, which is based in Wilmington, Massachusetts.

To some of my colleagues and students, especially at the Pratt Institute of Art and Design in New York, the Royal College of Art in London, and the New World School of the Arts in Miami, who for years have had to be patient with my critical eye, I offer my sincere apologies. Often their countless attempts to moderate their excessive use of computer graphics to solve visual and artistic problems has led me to ascertain the most creative way to use a computer.

For their continued support during this project I offer my sincere thanks to Terry and Enid Nolan-Woods.

It is impossible to give enough thanks here to my wife, Veronica, who has always encouraged me in my work and generously made time for this project by taking on the responsibilities of our two children, Marina and Marcus.

Introduction

Painting has reclaimed the territory it lost in 1839 when the invention of photography made Paul Delaroche declare "From today painting is dead." Today the marriage of electronic paint systems and digital photography is bridging the gap between painting and photography. In the last ten years digital images have turned the history of imagemaking on its head by making a photograph as plastic and changeable as a painting.

The history of photography has always followed the path of technological developments. When photogravure was introduced in the middle of the nineteenth century it enabled periodicals and books to use pictures. Then push button cameras and fast printing papers made the technology available to everyone. Industrial and commercial applications have even influenced the size and shape of photographs. Business and industry today also drive the evolution of new technology; as prices of software and hardware drop and performance, user interface, and output get better, the old preconceived boundaries between art and technology will fade away.

Conventional photography is a linear process that involves exposure, development, and printing. Digital images have specific advantages over material ones. They can be transmitted, manipulated, and stored easily. The veracity of the photograph disapears with the malleable quality of a digital picture.

Photography has never told the truth anyway — it has always been the photographer who framed the picture and chose the viewpoint. This is an evolutionary process not a revolutionary one. Artists and photographers have been collaging, airbrushing, solarizing, retouching, and vignetting for over a hundred years. Many definable qualities of digital photo illustration were anticipated by artists. Photomontage emerged in the nineteenth century and became a powerful tool in the hands of artists like Heartfield, Rodchenko, and Moholy Nagy.

By 1993 two generations of artists and designers have soaked in the glare of television. Images on a screen form our knowledge of the world today. As a result much digital photo illustration presents us with work that is conceptual and secondhand, and like many images from the mass media this genre already has a powerful hold on human perceptions.

Working with a computer enables the individual to interact with the raw material of our culture directly. Digital photo illustration is an attempt to secure the freedom of artistic expression in an effort to overcome what is in danger of becoming an everyday electronic style.

All image processing systems are founded on the same idea. Any picture, whether it is a drawing, a painting, or a photograph, can be turned into the binary data understood by a computer. With enough computer power this data can be manipulated easily. It is obvious that all graphic production is quickly becoming part of a big electronic chain. When artists put down their pencils and storyboards and begin working with the computer, physical production will no longer be managed by production craftspeople. The physical production process will have begun the moment the image is created. However, digital image processing still remains a post-creative production process. Even though the computer opens up a wealth of creative potential, few people have come to grips with approaching it in this way. Digital photo illustration looks at the processes and methods that can be used to exploit this potential.

The ease with which image processing systems can change existing images challenges ideas about what constitutes an "original" art work. Digital photo illustrations are rapidly destroying our concept of what an original is. Once a collection of picture elements are in the database of an image processing system, they can be manipulated without the loss of image quality known as "generation loss." With a digital image processing system, a copy is no longer inferior to the image it was based upon or copied from. The system also automatically retains a copy when the image is output, and so it is possible to archive these copies. An image can be output again at a later date, and that image will be identical to the one approved the first time, months or even years earlier. What remains in storage is actually less fugitive than a conventional photographic duplicate. The impact of digital image processing and copyright is being discussed in Washington. The Congressional Office of Technology currently is looking at the effect of technology on intellectual property. When these guidelines are completed, how will they affect the operator using the computer? Will any of this work be considered "original"?

M a r t h a   R o s l e r

Image Simulations, Computer Manipulations: Some Considerations

Pick a picture, any picture. The question at hand is the danger posed to "truth" by computer-manipulated photographic imagery.[1] How do we approach this question in a period in which the veracity of even the "straight," unmanipulated photograph has been under attack for a couple of decades?[2] Think of how much time has been spent in that period on the relation between the photographic "map" and an instant of past time. Think about Sergei Eisenstein and his development of filmic montage, which could extend and multiply the power of an instant. Now consider (an image of) the pyramids. If a photograph represents mutability, then surely the pyramids themselves are the very image of immutability—the immutability of objects. Necropolitan skyscrapers, they symbolize a death culture; they represent the staying power of something that yet decays, that will not last as long as the earth. Unlike the blasted ruins of the Acropolis, they are, moreover, brute geometry, enduring monuments to a long-eclipsed power of command over labor in a land now reduced to dry dust. Like

Ayers Rock in the middle of Australia, the pyramids represent another people's relation to the earth itself, about which we are nervously aware that we are largely unaware. Now think about moving the pyramids—as a whim, casually.

"Technology" makes it possible to move the pyramids photographically with hardly any trouble. Now, before we proceed with moving them, be forewarned that critical considerations of the possibilities of photographic manipulation tend to end with a tolling of the death knell for "truth." This discussion will not end that way.[3] It's possible that certain modes of address are near exhaustion as ways of communicating "facticity," but that doesn't amount to asserting either that "truth is dead" or that "photography is used up." Any familiarity with photographic history shows that manipulation is integral to photography. Over and above the cultural bias toward "Renaissance space" that provides the conceptual grounding of photography itself, there are the constraints of in-camera framing, lenses, lighting, and filtration. In printing an image, the selection of paper and other materials affects color or tonality, texture, and so forth. Furthermore, elements of the pictorial image can be suppressed or emphasized, and elements from other "frames" can be reproduced on or alongside them. And context, finally, is determining. (For linguistic context, there is the ubiquitous caption, for visual context, the multiplicative effect of images placed together; recall also the early Soviet film maker Lev Kuleshov's experiments in the influence of sequence on meaning in film.)

In the mid-nineteenth century, Oscar Rejlander concocted photographic montages that intrigued Queen Victoria. (If street urchins could be seen in interior doorways, and painters could represent them, why not photographers, despite the technical inability of photography to allow them to do so? If the representation of a dreamer and his dream can be thought, why could it not be presented photographically?) Charles Darwin, impressed by Rejlander's simulations, engaged him to prepare photographic representations of facial expressions of emotion from terror to loathing.[4] (The distinction between representation and falsification was not of interest here, and Rejlander's photos, in contrast to less staged or unstaged images in the same book, look Victorian, theatrical, Rejlanderesque.)

Nineteenth-century rural Americans apparently might have had trouble distinguishing between photographs of dead people as records of their bodies and as repositories of some portion of their souls; by the twentieth century this distinction had become a litmus test of civilization. In a less mystical, more practical vein, any nineteenth-century photographer of landscapes was likely to make good exposures of cloud-bearing skies to marry to appropriate images of the terrain below (or to retouch or double-expose the negatives), simply because orthochromatic film couldn't do justice to both at once. The great attention paid to skies in landscape painting had prepared the way for photographic skies to appear as presence, not as absence. So any outdoor photo was likely to be a montage, posing no problems of veracity for maker or viewer. All these manipulations were in the service of an undeniably truer truth, one closer to conceptual adequacy.

The identification of photography with objectivity is a modern idea, and the fascination with the precision of its rendering has only partly characterized its reception. Certainly the artistic practice of photography incorporated markers of the effort to evade the mechanicity of "straight" photography. The deceptive manipulation of images is another matter. The use of faked photographs is a long-standing political trick, in the form both of photographs misappropriated or changed after they were produced and in ones set up for the camera. Before 1880, when lithography enabled newspapers to use photographs directly, photographs were at the mercy of the engravers who prepared the printing plates for reproduction. Even now, cropping and airbrushing are effective methods of manipulating existing imagery, and set-up or staged ("restaged") images are always a likely possibility.

Restaging or faking is always an issue in war photography. Even "the most famous war photograph," Robert Capa's image of a soldier falling in battle in the Spanish Civil War, has been called a fake (partly because there is another Capa image that is strikingly similar).[5] In America, the emblematic photograph of World War II, Associated Press photographer Joe Rosenthal's Pulitzer Prize-winning image of marines raising a huge flag at Iwo Jima, was widely reputed to be a fraud. Despite the existence of photos of the original event by marine photographer Louis Lowery, the statue at the Marine Corps War Memorial at Arlington is based on Rosenthal's image. The restaging was in the interest of

Marine Corps public relations, and both groups of men—those who had raised the original, smaller flag during combat and those who had taken part in the restaging—were repeatedly made to lie about the event, and the restagers, not those who had really raised the flag, and Rosenthal, not Lowery, were honored.[6] Earlier, and with less consequence, in the American Civil War, Timothy O'Sullivan, in Matthew Brady's employ, is believed to have moved at least one body.[7] By the Spanish-American War of 1898, when news images had routinely (if recently) become photographic, newsreel photographers were re-creating important scenes such as the taking of San Juan Hill in Cuba or the battle in the harbor below, famously restaged in a bathtub. Journalistic veracity and, more sophisticatedly, objectivity—the absence of an invested point of view—are concepts born of the early twentieth century, vexed responses of the newspaper industry to the crises of political journalism—particularly war reportage, and particularly of the Spanish-American War.

In early newsreels, meant as entertainment, events such as important prize fights might be restaged for the camera, with painted spectators as backdrop. In the infancy of corporate photography, which has burgeoned into brochure production, images of manufacturing plants were routinely adjusted to get rid of dirt, damp, decay, and any other form of intrusive ugliness detracting from the nascent image of the manufactory as one grand machine. And Playboy, airbrushing its nudes in the interest of a more perfect vision of an ideal bedroom appliance, was simply following custom. Commerce and entertainment still provide the most widely accepted rationales for manipulation.

In producing images of proposed buildings, architects not willing to forgo the superior veracity suggested by the photograph might go to Hedrich-Blessing, a photographic firm that pioneered in the stripping together of negatives.[8] The final image blended the architect's model of his building with the proposed site so skillfully that clients couldn't tell that they were looking at something Walt Disney's "Imagineers" might have conjured up. Were the clients fooled? Less than visitors to Disneyland. Not fooling people but selling them was the idea, as in the rest of advertising, where reality is adjusted. Magic-show illusionism done with the proverbial smoke and mirrors helped spur the invention of filmic projection and movies.[9] Daguerre himself was a showman whose business depended on the two-dimensional re-creation of architectonic space (though most likely a space already known, but only through pictorial representation or verbal description) and its "placement" in time through the manipulation of light.[10] It can, finally, be argued, as does the critic Janet Abrams, that all architectural photography fictionalizes because it "prepares one only for the optimum conditions, not just the building newborn . . . but the building severed neatly from its surroundings, the building always sunbathing . . . smiling for the camera."[11]

In the late 1980s, while digitizing technology was being developed, there was still a lucrative market niche for spectacularly manipulated images produced in the old-fashioned, in-camera way; photo magazines tended to feature their makers once a month. For example, in 1988 the first issue of Kodak's high-gloss promotional magazine Studio Light, aimed at commercial photographers, led with the "special effects" photography of Kansas City photographer Michael Radencich.[12] Radencich specialized in Star Wars-like corporate images, each produced through the use of hand-made table-top (often paper) models and multiple exposures, on a single sheet of Ektachrome 64 Professional Film. Radencich stresses the need for "believability."[13] So much has changed since 1988, not only for image production but for Kodak! But, in the interim, although most such trick photos have become likely to be made without being physically staged, the point to note is that the technology is following a cultural imperative rather than vice versa.

IMAGE INTERVENTION VIA COMPUTER

When National Geographic abridged the space between one pyramid and another on its cover for February 1982, was it betraying its (believing) public? Earlier, I harped on the reading of the pyramids as a symbol of immutability and control. If we move them photographically, are we betraying history? Are we asserting the easy dominion of our civilization over all times and all places, as signs that we casually absorb as a form of loot? For their April 1982 cover, the Geographic adjusted the emblem on a Polish soldier's hat, importing it from another frame in the photographer's roll of film. These perhaps inconsequential changes have provoked a small but persistent fuss. The Geographic was using computerized digitizing technology, which converts an image into minuscule "pixels" (a neologism for "picture elements") that can be adjusted at will. To move a pyramid with the use of a computer seems to some to be more innocent than moving it, say, by stripping negatives or making photomontages, where the brute act of combination requires the handling of materials and their physical separation by cutting, not just rearranging of "information." To others it seems, for that very reason, more suspect and dangerous. The Geographic apparently isn't above using staged photos, though presumably the staging is done at the initiative of the photographers, not by editorial directive, for the imperative is to get that picture, no excuses. The fact that this occasions small comment underlines the point.[14]

When I described the basics of computer manipulation of photographs to a California law officer, his immediate response was, "That would mean the end of photographs as evidence." The consequences of undermining the credibility of photographic legal evidence shouldn't be underestimated, but the issue is more complex than it might appear and that discussion is beyond the compass of this article.[15] I consider the matter briefly further on. In journalism—where standards of evidence are more nebulous but of great interest nonetheless—observers are worried that digitizing technology will be used to "fix up" news photos. Once again, the journalistic profession is attempting to close ranks against overt manipulation in order to protect its reputation and the basis of its license to practice. The fears about digitization center on the ease and availability of digitizing equipment. Such machinery, pioneered by Scitex, Hell, and Crosfield, is part of the equipment used to produce many newspapers and magazines.[16] The controversy centers on news images, since magazines (and feature sections of newspapers, such as food, fashion, and other "lifestyle" or "business" sections) have often made use of set-up images as well as manipulated and retouched photographs. The rationale is that the visual appeal and cleanliness (so to speak) of images, not photographic accuracy, are the criteria in these uses. But "interpretive" representations in which elements are literally manipulated—either before or after the photograph is made—are anathema to photojournalists, publicly at any rate.

IMAGE CONTROL OR INFORMATION CONTROL?

When a U.S. art critic gave a talk at a photographic "congress" on a well-known artist whose practice was built solely upon appropriated mass media (in fact, advertising) photos, the response was volcanic.[17] The audience's worst nightmares, it seemed, had never thrown up a practice such as the critic described. The proprietary relation of the professional photographers who were present to their images was made very clear when the photographers threatened physical doom to any artist found appropriating their work. No surprise, then, that they expressed general support for the then-pending congressional amendment, sponsored by the aggressively right-wing Congressman Jesse Helms of North Carolina, to withhold public funding from art work deemed obscene or otherwise offensive—an initiative that expressed in extreme form the collective Imaginary's fear and loathing of artists, and, in fact, of photographers. Of art photographers, that is— the same people whom professional ("working") photographers fear and loathe (or at least loathe) for their lack of respect for the unmediated image.

I remarked earlier that art photography perpetually defines itself by stressing its distance from the recording apparatus; it often does so by relying on arcane theories of vision and on manipulation of the print, more recently on conceptual or critical-theoretical grounding. In the eyes of professional photographers, this no doubt makes art photographers unskilled charlatans, loose cannons who get rich by fleecing the public. Such "working" photographers, fixing their horizon at the level of copyright, are in no position to see that artists' motivations for appropriating photojournalistic and other workaday photographic images are not so far from their own fears of manipulation; the difference, of course, is that the artists see commercial photography and photojournalism as deeply implicated in the processes of social manipulation while the producers of the images are more likely to see themselves as at the mercy of those who control the process.[18] Autonomy for each is the underlying theme.

While professional photographers stop at the level of ownership of the image, the future lies with the conversion of the image to "information," making photographers, no matter how souped up, chip-laden, automated, and expensive their still cameras are, look like little ol' craftsmen or cowboys, cranky remnants of the old petit bourgeoisie. In 1986, American Photographer magazine reported on an effort by a bunch of business-school whiz kids to create a stock-image bank in digital form with their newly formed National Digital Corporation (ndc). The article, by Anne M. Russell, treated the effort with suspicion, remarking that the stock-image business is low-profit and NDC, while acknowledging that supplying those images would represent only a third of their business, declined to specify what the other two-thirds would be, citing only unstated government archives; and several similar but less ambitious efforts in the early 1980s had already foundered. She concluded: "The toughest test of the system will not be the technical one, however; it will be whether [it] can win converts in an industry that so far has demonstrated little love for technology beyond the camera."[19] I'll say. But digitized stock-image banks are inevitable. In her 1986 article Russell makes no mention of the hazards of the loss of control of the image's visual appearance— that is, of its conversion into information. And, once it has become information (which every hacker, unlike every photographer or telecommunications manager, or every computer executive, believes should, by definition, be free), both sellers and buyers will have to pay for access.

Although NDC's dream of work stations in offices across the country may not yet have been realized, the fact is that every newspaper of any size now has the Scitex-type digitizing technology in its make-up room, despite its considerable cost.[20] This increases the likelihood that decisions to alter photos will be made casually, by those liable to slight the niceties of photojournalistic ethics. Presently the primary newspaper use of this technology for images is in adjusting color and "burning and dodging" as in traditional black-and-white darkroom procedures. (The newspaper USA Today tells its photographers what kind of film to use for given situations, regardless of the lighting source, and removes the hues produced by fluorescent lighting by recoloring. Other newspapers also do this.[21]) The nightmare of photojournalists, who remember that W. Eugene Smith quit Life magazine (twice) over its editors' intention to use some of his photos in ways he didn't appreciate, is that some editor somewhere will start by adjusting the color or diminishing the clutter in some image and go on to a career of photographic alteration. Tom Hubbard, in News Photographer magazine, recounts the routine "dialing in" by an engraver of the color blue for a swimming pool photo in the

Orange County Register illustrating a story about vandals dyeing the water red(!)[22] Here the change was not editorial but technical and "inadvertent," but it's just the kind of egregious error that makes photographers and ethicists wince.

Newspaper photo editors, when asked, uniformly reject retouching or other forms of manipulating photos, claiming that even flopping photos is not allowed, so why would they acquiesce in more pernicious changes? On the other hand, U.S. television network executives have been more positive about the possibilities of photo retouching of all sorts. (There seem to be no "picture editors" on TV.) They describe removing elements in photos and footage, for instance microphones in front of speakers, or straightening of presidential candidates' shoulders (but supposedly not their faces).[23]

But in the newspaper field, photojournalists and even newspaper picture editors are still interested in obtaining assurances from management that they won't do what the editors of the Geographic (and of Newsweek's puff series on various countries called "A Day in the Life of . . . "[24] have seen fit to do)—to "improve" their pictures for the sake of conceptual accuracy, aesthetic pleasure, formatting, hucksterism, and so forth. Yet they are well aware that photographs have been subject to change, distortion, and misuse since the beginning of photographic time. The simplest misrepresentation of a photograph is its use out of context. The most remarked-on examples are, of course, political, and prominently feature examples related to war. War photographers Susan Meiselas and Harry Mattison have exhibited photos they have taken of atrocities in El Salvador and events in Nicaragua that they claim had been clearly labeled but that have been intentionally misused by journalistic outlets. The misuse has included lies about what is being shown, when, who did it, and what it "means."

HARD EVIDENCE

Photographic exhibits of documentary evidence provide another arena of exploitation. Senator Joseph McCarthy made liberal use of "damning" photographs and charts in his anti-Communist crusade, and in one celebrated instance—captured in Emile De Antonio and Daniel Talbot's wonderful film

Point of Order! (1963)—the exposure of McCarthy's use of a cropped photo provided a vehicle for his discrediting during the 1953 Army-McCarthy hearings. My favorite example of lying through the presentation of a photographic exhibit is the photo of mysterious cargo—as used, for example, by President Ronald Reagan in exposing the public via television to a blurry photo of "Nicaraguan Sandinista official Tomás Borge loading drugs" (cocaine) onto or unloading them from a small plane on an obscure airstrip in "Nicaragua." This line of evidence is one of the CIA disinformation mill's favorites. Blurry aerial photos, virtually incomprehensible without decoding, were used to very powerful effect in the Cuban missile crisis.[25] It seems that no matter how much we don't believe the media, such exhibits always give doubters pause. Maybe.

Years ago, writer Susan Sontag expressed righteous anger over the political manipulation of photographs by Chinese authorities. Her cases in point included the removal of the suddenly hated Chang Ching from a venerated image of Mao on the Long March. Such maneuvers point to the authoritarian manipulativeness of the regime, but they appear most of all to be a neatening up of historical representations that have a largely ceremonial function, in a society unlikely to base its conceptions of social meaning on photography in quite the ways ours does. In a widely noted example of the misuse of an apparently straightforward documentary photograph—one more recent and closer to home—early in the Reagan administration Secretary of State Alexander Haig waved a photo of a body on fire. He called it an image of a Miskito Indian being burned after a Sandinista massacre, and cited it as evidence of Sandinista brutality. In fact, this photo, which he obtained from a right-wing French magazine, was of a body being burned by Red Cross workers—who were cropped out of the photo—during the uprising against Somoza.[26] The image was meant to be decisive in rallying support for the still-secret war in Nicaragua. In this instance the original photo could be located, and perhaps its negative could be found as well.

In digitization, there may be no original, no negative—only copies, only "information." Certainly, as the image emerges from digitization, it is not via a "negative"; the final image has no negative. Perhaps even more troublesome is the fact that electronic still cameras (produced by several Japanese manufacturers such as Canon, Sony, and Fuji, with others promised from other manufacturers) can bypass the production of film, negatives, and prints, and feed their information directly into a computer.[27] Once the images are in the computer, it is more likely that technicians rather than photographers or editors will monitor their fate.

If we want to call up hopeful or positive uses of manipulated images, we must choose images in which manipulation is itself apparent, and not just as a form of artistic reflexivity but in order to make a larger point about the truth value of photographs and the illusionistic elements in the surface of (and even the definition of) "reality." (I don't mean a generalized or universal point alone but ones about particular, concrete situations and events.) Here we must make the requisite bow to Brecht's remark about the photo of the exterior of the Krupp works not attesting to the conditions of slavery within. The origins of photomontage as an aesthetic-political technique are not certain, but the Dadaists used it to disrupt the smooth, seamless surface of quotidian urban existence. John Heartfield still provides an unsurpassed example of political photomontage. In the 1930s, Heartfield, employing painstaking techniques and a sizable staff, produced photomontages with integral texts for the left-wing mass-circulation magazine Arbeiter-Illustrierte Zeitung (Worker-Illustrated Journal), or AIZ. In every photomontage was the implicit message that photography alone cannot "tell the truth" and also the reminder that fact itself is a social construction. This is not meant to deny that photographs provide some sort of evidence, only to suggest that the truth value of photography is often overrated or mislocated.

THE DIGITIZATION MARKET

Digitization techniques, based on previously developed, more direct forms of image manipulation, are pervasive in commercial fields of visual illustration. They are used in the production of television commercials, music videos, and still-image advertisements (which may or may not be based on traditionally produced photographs), and they are the backbone of "desk-top publishing."[28] Digitization and still-video imaging are finding new corporate uses in financial, training, sales, and marketing presentations.[29] In medicine, digitized imaging, particularly in conjunction with CAT scans and ultrasound, has produced a new type of representation of the inside of the body.[30] Ultrasound imaging, particularly of developing fetuses, is now widely recognizable, and this potent representation has been of use to anti-abortion forces. For the home market—interested not in strict accuracy but in prestige-enhancing aesthetic values, in landscape, tourism, and above all in portraiture—ordinary color labs now may purchase an Agfa CRT printer (still in limited production) that offers image enhancement in making prints from slides, from the increase of sharpness and reduction of grain to the removal of "unwanted features, such as shadows."[31]

Computer animation techniques have been used to combine photographic and drawn imagery in films, such as Disney's Tron (1982). After the popular apocalypto-shoot-'em-up Terminator II (1991) used an advanced computer-animated image-metamorphosis technique, it was featured so heavily in television commercials that its novelty value was quickly exhausted. The TV news directors who were enthusiastic about light retouching of non-facial stills also claimed to have produced simulated moving footage of political personalities, but never to have put such simulations on the air. In an instance of non-news simulation of dead personalities—or, one should say, of "icons" —in the six-minute videotape Rendez-vous à Montréal (1987) Humphrey Bogart and Marilyn Monroe were computer animated.[32] Although the characters, based on small sculptural models, are blatant caricatures, and their movements and voices bizarrely unlifelike, lawyers for the Bogart estate have reportedly threatened to sue the videotape's makers, Nadia Magnenat-Thalmann and Daniel Thalmann. The Thalmanns, who operate under the nom de computation The Human Factory, were computer instructors at the University of Montreal business school at the time they produced this and similar animations. Their ventures have been funded by the Québec provincial government and a number of institutions and corporations from Kodak to Bell Canada and Northern Telecom. Daniel Thalmann, according to the Dallas Morning News, has said, "I think that within five years, one won't be able to tell the difference between a real person on film and one created by the Human Factory," and, "Soon, a film may no longer be accepted as proof that something happened." The first question we might ask is, under what circumstances is a film acceptable now as proof that something happened? The Morning News also quotes Daniel Thalmann as claiming that "you won't need real people any more. . . Actors could be out of a job."[33] The second question to ask is, when can a film be taken as displaying "real people"? These are not empty questions to be considered.

As Thalmann's remarks suggest, the discussion of the effects of computerization on modern society tends to bifurcate: either the concern is with the reception of computerized images and the effects on society as a whole, or it is with the impact of computerization on production and the experience of labor—the classic split between production and consumption, in which the latter is universalized and the former demoted, at best to a technicality and at worst to an inconvenience. Jean Baudrillard dismisses George Orwell's vision of the video screen as a Big Brother surveillance monitor because, following Hans Magnus Enzensberger (with whom he agrees about nothing else), he notes that television has already prevented people from talking to one another—so there is no possibility of significant subversion to monitor. "There is no need to imagine it as a state periscope spying on everyone's private life—the situation as it stands is more efficient than that: it is the certainty that people are no longer speaking to each other, that they are definitively isolated in the fact of a speech without response."[34] As usual, this leaves out the question of the relation of the screen to productive labor.

COMPUTERIZATION AND THE PROCESSES OF LABOR

The development of digital image-processing techniques will most immediately affect the status of those who work with still images—particularly of photographers. As I suggested earlier, it opens the way for a further loss of relative autonomy for the professional photographer, who may become, like the TV news–camera operator, merely a link in the electronic chain of command. Kodak is marketing a sensor capable of high-resolution digital imaging that couples with a conventional Nikon F3 camera body. This device, which sells for about $20,000, captures images that can be easily transmitted by satellite or wire, making the still photographer part of the "electronic newsroom." According to Fortune, in 1989 a CNN photographer using a similar device bypassed censors by surreptitiously sending an image of a Tienanmen Square demonstrator via telephone. But there is a wider application for computerization than image conversion, and the computer's effects on the working environment apply far beyond the bounds of photography.

Consider some of the effects of computerization on work in general—both the changed nature of the work itself and new hazards associated with it, both physical and personal, hazards such as loss of autonomy in the work process and loss of privacy because of monitoring. Computerization is well entrenched in productive-labor (nonoffice) processes, in the form of machine-shop computer-control applications and sophisticated three-dimensional drafting and modeling.[35] Computer-enhanced imaging has also altered the face of the graphics industry, turning graphic artists into computer operators. This has wrought changes not only in the types and level of skills (and capitalization) such artists require but also in the nature and locale of their work. Virtually all computer jobs (despite Baudrillard's assertion about the television set, which he considers as the site of reception, not production) also contain the possibility of absolute and effortless surveillance, as well as ever-expanding forms of Taylorism—time-and-motion "study" or efficiency-expert management. Since computers have the inherent ability to monitor all work done on them, the number of keystrokes per hour of computer operators can be effortlessly monitored, or surveilled. And it is, as all observers have reported.[36]

A large proportion of workers affected by computerization—and by monitoring—are women, so-called "pink-collar workers."[37] The women's clerical workers' union 9 to 5 began reporting on health problems associated with video display terminals, or VDT's, in the 1970s, and it has more recently considered the issues associated with monitoring.[38] By the 1980s, concern about hazards associated with computer use among workers (now including white-collar workers, including those in the newsroom—that is, reporters, was so widespread that Congress looked into it.[39]

The hazards of the machinery are in some ways like and in other ways quite unlike those posed by earlier types of machinery developed since the Industrial Revolution. Reporters, for example, are more worried about carpal-tunnel syndrome or repetitive strain injuries (keyboard-related injuries resulting from repetitive motion) and other health effects than they are about surveillance, since the story, not the keystroke, is their measure of productivity. The Newspaper

Guild has been studying VDTs since the early 1970s, but the repetitive strain injuries, which are more characteristic of industrial labor (and even of such activities as hand knitting), were an unlooked-for result of the use of keyboards, not video display terminals.[40]

Meanwhile, new fears among computer users include the potential hazards of electromagnetic emissions from terminals.[41] This is a result of the more general reawakening of concern over extremely low frequency (ELF) magnetic fields, which are generated by all electrical sources, from high-voltage power lines to all household appliances, from toasters to TVs. Late in 1989 the Congressional Office of Technology Assessment (OTA) released a report that concluded that there was "legitimate reason for concern" about the biological effects of ELF, but that also stated that there was no research basis for asserting a significant risk.

To return to the graphics industry: Computerization reduces the number of technologies involved in production and allows the workforce to be dispersed, with the work often done in the artists' own homes—which might be in Asia. This reversion to "home work" (not in the school sense but as the term has been used in sweated industries like garment production) fragments the labor force, making not only conversation but also solidarity close to impossible, producing a more docile group of piece workers, who as independent contractors also generally lose all their nonwage benefits, such as health insurance, paid vacations, sick leave, and pensions. The ability to work at home is often treated as a social advance, but in most such discussions the people affected are executive or managerial in rank; the effects on lower-level or shop-floor employees are slighted, if not celebrated for producing labor peace. In arguing for the repeal of labor laws that prohibit piece work, the defense of these new forms of homework for production workers has been disingenuously couched in terms of rural or small-town craftswomen sewing for a living while tending the homestead.

THE CULTURE OF SIMULATION

The decline of industrial labor and its system of valuation and workforce organization (and self-organization), and the development of a culture whose common currency is the production of images and signs, constitutes the burden of

Baudrillard's arguments about simulation, which have provided so much grist for contemporary critical mills. Yet, as with Baudrillard's precursor and intellectual mentor Marshall McLuhan, recognition of the media's power to flatten both experience and difference has led to capitulation or (more in the case of Baudrillard than McLuhan) to cynicism. Baudrillard, along with many of his followers, believes that truth is no longer an issue, since all signs are interchangeable. He writes that, for example, the subject of every single thing that appears on television is "you": "YOU are news, you are the social, the event is you, you are involved, you can use your voice, etc. . . . No more violence or surveillance; only information, secret virulence, chain reaction, slow implosion, and simulacra of spaces where the real-effect again comes into play."[42] The problem with such totalizing pessimism is that it provides an adequate description of neither causes nor real-life experiences. It remains a fantasy of power of those implicated in the system of production of signification. Yet we cannot dismiss the tendencies toward "implosion" of meaning and the difficulty of distinguishing the real from the artificial that Baudrillard describes, following a line of thinkers that includes not just McLuhan but Frankfurt School cultural critics Adorno and Horkheimer and Walter Benjamin, as well as Gunther Anders and the French situationists, notably Guy Debord. In 1967 Debord opened Part I, "Separation Perfected," of his immensely influential book La société du spectacle with the following quotation:

> But certainly for the present age, which prefers the sign to the thing signified, the copy to the original, fancy to reality, the appearance to the essence . . . illusion only is sacred, truth profane. Nay, sacredness is held to be enhanced in proportion as truth decreases and illusion increases, so that the highest degree of illusion comes to be the highest degree of sacredness.[43]

This quotation is from Ludwig Feuerbach's preface to the second edition of The Essence of Christianity, published in German in 1841.[44] Feuerbach's remark is taken as an early diagnosis of a trend that has since become all-pervasive. Well, then, what shall we think about computer-processed imagery, which may indeed produce copies with no "original," and about its relation to photographic documentation?

Earlier I invoked the pyramids and the cultural transactions involved in photographing them and electronically adjusting their placement on the land. In

Jean-Luc Godard's anti-imperialist, anti-war movie Les Carabinières, the main characters, tattered simpletons named something like Michelangelo and Raphael (not after the turtles), return home to their wives after a grotesque national military adventure. "We bring you all the treasures of the world," they proclaim, opening a suitcase and pulling out card after card picturing monuments and wonders. In 1992, the United Nations Educational, Scientific and Cultural Organization (UNESCO) announced a plan to photograph 200 "cultural and natural wonders" of the world and to make the images "instantly available worldwide through digital transmission," according to the New York Times.[45] This UNESCO adventure, called Projet Patrimoine 2001, is backed financially by the immensely rich La Caixa Foundation (supported by Barcelona's municipal pension funds), which donated $140 million for the first year.[46] Technical services will be provided by Kodak, France Telecom, and the Gamma photo agency. Selected sites, to be recorded with "scientific comprehensiveness and artistic beauty" in mind, will come from a UNESCO list of so-called world heritage sites. The idea is to make images of such treasures as Angkor Wat or the Seychelles Islands turtles, before, according to the Times, "they are further damaged by war or the environment." On a lesser scale, there are moves afoot in various cities, such as New York, to require that buildings slated for demolition be photographed beforehand (by process unspecified). One wonders whether the proponents of such measures know that such cataloguing was one of the earliest governmentally mandated uses of photography, as in Thomas Annan's documentation of slum sections of old Glasgow in the 1860s and 1870s before their demolition, the photographing of old Paris by Charles Marville in the 1860s before the implementation of Baron Haussmann's monumental boulevard plan, or Eugène Atget's records of "old Paris" at the turn of the twentieth century.[47] The relation to Godard's carabineers needs no further explication—but what of the idea of "capturing" something photographically and transmitting it in a medium that implies mutation and change? Of what value, precisely, will be the record assembled?

Perhaps it is time to return to the questions I raised about computer animator Daniel Thalmann's remarks—namely, when can we ever take film or photos to represent real events or real people? Earlier I referred to the endangerment by digitization of one of photography's quotidian uses, that of the provision of courtroom evidence. Granted, with respect to publishing, all publishers of whatever size should be assumed to be in possession of image-processing equipment and all publications to be produced by one computerized process or another. But these elements of the labor process are not prominent in the public consciousness. What will affect public attitudes, however, are imaging products soon to be available for the mass market. Companies are devoting a great deal of attention to developing such products at acceptable cost. These will likely provide customers with multiple possibilities for viewing, from "hard copies" to television-screen images, and the information will be stored in a variety of ways—on video disks, tape, or, most likely, compact disks. Images will be manipulable with varying degrees of ease. As the public becomes used to the idea of the image as data in flux, the believability of photographic images—the common assumption that a photo is true unless shown to be otherwise—will likely wane. (But we have also to acknowledge that outside the judicial process [one hopes], the perverse tenacity of the will to fantasy, the fantasy that sells the National Enquirer, the Weekly World News, and People magazine images we have discussed, fantasy that requires the act of faith that photos do not lie. Period.)

There are social costs associated with the radical delegitimization of photography. Although such delegitimization would make it more difficult for state officials to wave photos around as evidence of this or that, clearly it also diminishes the public circulation of communications of factuality. The development of a politically active citizenry depends on the ability to receive and communicate information about events and situations not directly experienced, including the experiences of others. Even without the collapse of photographic legitimacy, merely reproducing documentary images can rarely mobilize or even, perhaps, inform. Without an adequate discussion of the context and meaning of the social relations represented, such images cannot work, unless the audience already shares certain presumptions about "what things mean."[48] Like the photo of the Krupp works, such documents are accurate but insufficient. The question, then, is not whether to manipulate images but how—and also how to use them straight to "tell the truth."

Rapid advances in digitization and other computer technologies will continue to alter modes of information delivery in specialized and general uses and will certainly transform not only photography but also the television, telephone, and personal computer industries. The present article is a palimpsest of arguments configured to conform to questions posed by the state of computerization of photography and other images. When I began writing in 1988, Kodak was still a "photo" company, making and marketing film, and the professional photography establishment was worrying about digitization of photos. As I write in 1992, digitization is taken for granted, and interest centers on the use of new, miniaturized digitization devices for photographers such as were used at the Olympics; on data compression that enables the transmission of digital video images by telephone (presently, fiber optic) lines; and on encryption.[49] In the first instance, tiny portable monitors and scanners return some measure of control in the field to the photographer. In the second, digitization and, importantly, compression of video images may well make broadcast television obsolete; the Supreme Court has granted the myriad Baby Bell phone companies the right to transmit video, in a service called "video dial tone." In the third instance, the transmission of images, and indeed of other data, has opened the possibility of tampering, so that corporate senders have urgently developed highly complex, virtually unbreakable forms of encryption. But the government is opposing such encryption, because it does not wish to allow any entity to transmit data it cannot intercept and monitor at will. Meanwhile, the computer industry seeks resuscitation, searching desperately for a new industry-transformative device, whether it be keyboardless, cable-free, or even wearable computers.

THE LARGER PICTURE

These are the contexts for the manipulation of still photographs. In sum, concerns about manipulation center on political, ethical, judicial, and other legal issues (such as copyright), as well as the broader ideological ramifications of how a culture deploys "evidence" it has invested with the ability to bear ("objective") witness irrespective of the vicissitudes of history and personality. Complications posed by questions of reception, such as those raised by post-structuralist critics and philosophers, have themselves fueled a pessimism about the ability to communicate meaning (let alone "truth"). Nevertheless, as I've already indicated, it seems unreasonable to conclude that meaning cannot be communicated, let alone that "the photograph as evidence of anything is dead," to quote the Whole Earth Review's slightly hysterical discussion of digitized photography.[50] To be sure, newspapers, photographers, and governments should be enjoined, formally or informally, from changing elements of photographs that are presented as evidence of anything at all; but the idea of the photograph as raw evidence is one with a rather short history, and the erection of Potemkin villages for politics or entertainment neither began nor will end with the electronic manipulation of photographic imagery. That is not to say that an era characterized by certain beliefs and cultural practices is not passing in the West. A more general cultural delegitimization than the questioning of photographic truth is at work in the industrial societies. This delegitimization is as much a product of political failure as of image societies, and it entails the declining faith in the project of modernity and its religion of "progress." In describing its material basis (though not in his totalized conclusions), Debord was surely correct to locate the genesis of "the society of the spectacle" in the process of capitalist industrial production and the dominance of the commodity form—this despite Baudrillard's attempted correction of Debord's theory to the interchangeability not of commodities but of signs.[51]

There are productive aspects to the adoption of a skeptical relation to information provided by authorities. The real danger—as evidenced by the mass willingness of Americans to take refuge from uncertainty in the utterances of their leaders, regardless of the plethora of evidence contradicting them—is political; it is the danger that people will choose fantasy, and fantasy identification with power, over a threatening or intolerably dislocating social reality.[52]

As always, social meanings and their perception are not fully determined by the technologies used in their production but rather are circumscribed both by wider hegemonic ideological practices and by the practices and traditions of those who oppose them. If material conditions need to be redescribed, more painstakingly and in novel forms, in order to be reinvested with "believability," then we can surely develop the forms—and the means of dissemination—to do so.

Murray Oles

Input, Output, and Quality Control

With the birth of the Computer Age came one of its first acronyms, GIGO, "Garbage In Garbage Out." All too often, one reaches the end of a long hard job, and finds disappointment, even disaster, and the reason often comes down to "GIGO." You start with bad data, you end up with bad results.

In the digital world of art preparation, true results are not evident until the digital data is recorded in final analogue form. This is the worst time to learn that the process was doomed from the start. The purpose of this chapter is to provide some insight into the variables involved with inputting and outputting digital data to be used in the computer-assisted production of images.

As artists work with computers to produce art, it is essential to understand that the computer is only a toolbox. Properly organized and utilized, it can enable an artist to produce excellent results with great efficiency.

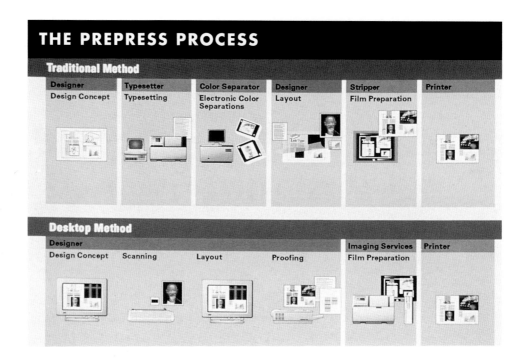

THE PREPRESS PROCESS

Traditional Method

Designer	Typesetter	Color Separator	Designer	Stripper	Printer
Design Concept	Typesetting	Electronic Color Separations	Layout	Film Preparation	

Desktop Method

Designer				Imaging Services	Printer
Design Concept	Scanning	Layout	Proofing	Film Preparation	

CONTROL PROCEDURES

Control procedures are an essential part of the process of understanding how the computer is operating. Controls help to identify problems at critical stages of the process, and, properly used, they can prevent an artist from wasting effort.

The best control item is a test image. Every prepress professional has his or her favorite test image, and despite their differences, all test images perform the same function. They establish standards by which comparisons are made throughout every step of a process.

A good test image should establish standards for gray balance, tone linearity, color linearity, sharpness, and resolution. A test image has to be measurable and must be archived in every format throughout the process.

Test images usually start with a studio photograph containing a gray scale and color scales for RGB and CMYK color spaces. To help identify linearity problems, continuous tone scales should be established alongside stepped off scales. If possible, reflective densitometry readings should be taken and written opposite each measured step.

CHOOSING AN ORIGINAL

Lighting Conditions

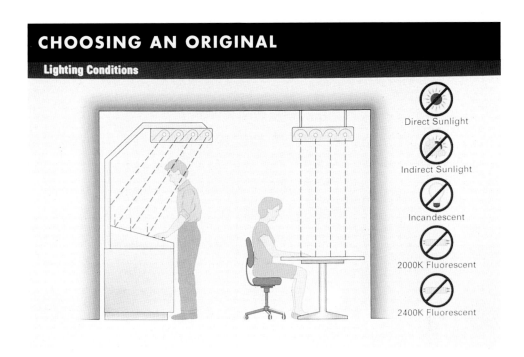

Direct Sunlight

Indirect Sunlight

Incandescent

2000K Fluorescent

2400K Fluorescent

PROCESS VARIABLES

The creation of digital data from some form of image is referred to as data capture, or input. There are several variables affecting the quality and accuracy of the input that must be controlled. The processing of digital data will also introduce process variables affecting the final image quality. Changes in size, angle, and color space are three common processes that can dramatically alter the quality of the end result.

Once all the data has been massaged digitally, it must be either transferred to another system, or converted to analogue data for recording onto film, paper, or some type of hard copy (electrostatically imaged printing plates, electrophotographically imaged xerographic proofers, electronically controlled ink jet nozzles or electronically addressed heat transfer elements).

Input, process, and output must all be controlled. When all the steps are under control, the artist can isolate every variable and identify its unique characteristics. The same principles apply in the conventional art world. The only difference is that with digital image processing, different tools are used.

DIGITAL DATA

Digital data, used in all computers, is a binary coding of information. The smallest binary code element is a bit. A bit can be either on or off. Obviously, a bit does not contain a great deal of information regarding tone, but it can tell a great deal about line work. On is black, off is white, or vice versa.

A byte is a collection of bits, and in most imaging systems today eight bits are used to make up one byte. Why eight? With eight on-off bits pulled together into a single word or byte, it is possible to code 256 different words, or bytes. When there are 256 different levels of tone, the human eye cannot discern a visual difference between the increments. In other words, a 256-level gray scale appears to the viewer to be a smooth gradation.

A byte can have more than eight bits, and some scanners capture as many as fourteen bits per color in order to extract the most accurate digital file from an image. Although fourteen bits are captured, most image processing systems work with eight bit bytes, and so the oversampled fourteen-bit word is resampled to produce an optimized eight bit byte.

A picture is described digitally as a bit map. A bit map is a matrix of pixels arranged on an X/Y grid. (The word pixel is an acronym for "Picture Element.") Imagine that you divided an image up into tiny little lines spaced so close together that three hundred lines were packed into each inch of the picture. Suppose that each one of these lines, each one three-hundredth of an inch thick, was segmented into tiny square segments also one three-hundredth of an inch deep. One square inch of an image would contain 90,000 squares of image pieces. One of these tiny squares is called pixel.

Each pixel in an image's bit map is described digitally by assigning a number of bits and bytes to it. The simplest form of describing an image is with a one bit byte per each pixel. In this manner a black and white line image can be described.

In order to describe an image with black and white tone, more bits per byte are necessary. A four bit byte can describe sixteen variations of tone from white to black. Eight bits can describe 256 gray levels. An image with 300 pixels per linear inch (90,000 pixels per square inch) containing eight bit pixels will look like a continuous-tone black and white image. If twenty-four bits are used to describe a pixel, and eight bits are assigned to describe the tone for each of the three primary additive colors, Red, Green, and Blue, a continuous-tone color image can be described by the bit map.

The combination of bits and bytes used to describe a pixel, along with the frequency of pixels in a bit map, determines an image's resolution.

FORMATS

Digital data in bit map form has to be packaged so that a computer knows how the bits in each pixel are to be distributed and displayed. This description usually precedes the bit map data and sits at the start of an image's file. The data used to describe the specifics of an image's bit map is called the *header* information.

Unfortunately, when companies invented their computer imaging systems there was no standard procedure to describe an image. Each company wrote its own *format.* Consequently, an image written in a specific format for one system has little chance of being read correctly by another system.

To get around this problem, translators have been written. Of course this means that a change is made to the data's format, and may also mean that the data's values are different. An example of this problem can be shown in the translation between Crosfield and Scitex. Both companies use 32 bits to describe a Cyan, Magenta, Yellow, and Black (CMYK) pixel. Crosfield orders their pixel CMYK, and when they relate their 256 gray levels to dot percentages they apply digital level 32 to 0% dot. Scitex orders their pixel YMCK, and they assign digital level 0 to 0% dot.

Other formats have limitations on how large a file can be. Pict files cannot exceed 4000 pixels square. Tiff files can be either CMYK or RGB, and eight, sixteen, twenty-four, or thirty-two bit. The artist must know the differences between formats, establish procedures respecting format, and maintain control over the process.

Just as there are few standards for how data headers are written and formatted, there are a number of physical devices designed to hold digital data. Hard disks, floppy disks, removable hard disks, magnetic tape, optical disks, and proms (Programmable read only memory, most often used to encrypt software on "dongles") are all unique devices designed to hold various amounts of digital data. A floppy disk can range in size from 3.5 inches to 8 inches, and it may have a paper case or a hard plastic case. Floppies can vary significantly in density. High-density floppies can hold twice as much data as low-density floppies, but they may not be readable in the floppy drive that is installed in your computer. Syquest cartridges are currently a popular form of medium volume removable digital storage. The most popular syquest cartridges are the forty-four megabyte variety, and many manufacturers offer drives that can accept the Syquest media. Optical disks of the 5.25 inch variety can be formatted in many different ways. They may be capable of holding 300 or 600 megabytes per side, and they may not be compatable with one another.

Several new forms of fixed and removable digital media are now under development, and standards are not expected soon.

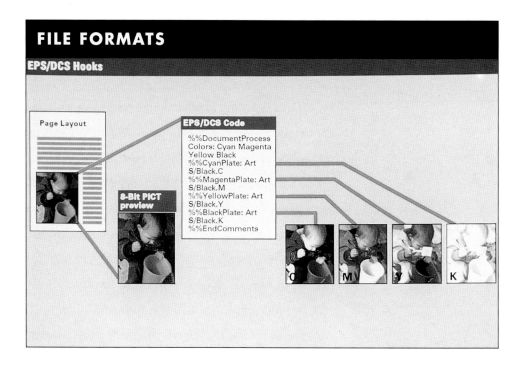

RESOLUTION

- -

Resolution, as described earlier, is the combination of bits and bytes used to describe a pixel, and the frequency of pixels in a bit map. The number of bits used to describe a color is as important as the density of pixels in a bit map. A more subtle resolution factor, but one that is equally important, is the quality of a pixel's color information.

Four eight-bit bytes, combined to form a pixel, will mathematically generate 16.7 million combinations. The caveat of which to be aware is in the input device's ability to distinguish equal differences in value, over all 256 levels, during image capture.

Photo sensors that convert light to electricity are used in scanners to capture images. The electrical pulses from a photo sensor are fed through an analogue to digital converter system (ADC). The ADC assigns the eight bits available to the incoming electrical pulses. Because photo sensors are nonlinear devices, this image-digitizing process can produce vastly different results. Hence the importance of proper calibration and the torough testing of all equipment used in image capture.

INTERPOLATION

Interpolation is used to convert a bit map in size, resolution, angle, color space, or sharpness. There are several mathematical formulas used to perform image interpolations. The quality of the interpolated image is directly affected by the sophistication of the interpolation algorithm used. More complex algorithms consider the image content by sampling larger areas of an image to identify contours. The more complex the algorithm, the longer the interpolation process.

Interpolation is not as good a method for changing size, resolution, or color space as is scanning. Wherever possible, avoid interpolating the original scanned bit map. If interpolation is going to be used, test it with an appropriate test image to verify that the results will be acceptable.

INPUT & IMAGE CAPTURE

Scanning

Scanning is a precise scientific process that demands calibration and control in order to achieve optimum results. The test image should be scanned on every color scanner that is used to capture images for the computer. The scanned test images should be saved on the computer's hard disk, and a backup copy should be archived and kept apart from the production disks.

The output of the test image's digital data completes the test process, and provides the benchmark by which all comparisons are made. Every type of output device should be tested with the standard digital data. Color separations, chromes, and digital proofs may all appear to be different, but at least evidence has been established to help provide accurate predictions of output results.

When testing new input scans for accuracy, compare the known test image to the new scan of the test image by viewing and examining both on the computer screen. Whenever possible, especially when new circumstances are introduced, the test image should be run through every step of the planned process. This includes opening the image up in any application programs to be used, saving the image in the applicable format, and plotting the image on the intended output. Save the data in each format through which it is transformed, so that any variations can be pinpointed to the exact point in the process where the change occurred.

There are three primary types of scanners in use today—drum scanners, flat bed scanners, and digital cameras.

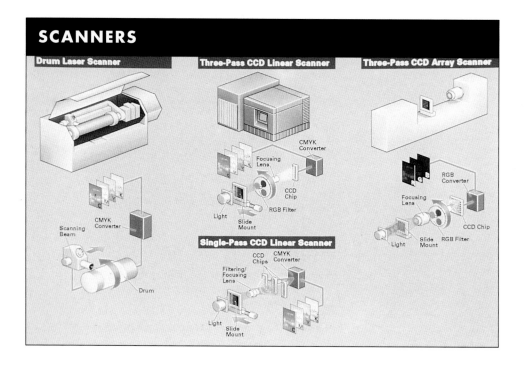

Drum Scanners

Drum scanners were the first means of image capture, and they have been highly developed over the past twenty years. In a drum scanner, an image is mounted mechanically onto a rotating cylinder that is placed on a lathe bed. The cylinder rotates, and a beam of light traverses the surface of the image. The beam either passes through the image that has been mounted on clear plastic cylinder, or reflects off the surface, as when it scans paper prints.

The beam of light is directed onto a photo sensor where a modulating electrical signal is created. The electrical signal is fed through the ADC circuitry and the resulting data is modified through Look Up Tables (LUT) and filters to correct its color, gray balance, sharpness, and in the case of a CMYK scanner, its black printer. Drum scanners have extremely high-resolution scanning capability, and they can be adjusted optically to sample a spot of light as small as ten microns in diameter.

Drum scanners are mechanical devices. They need constant maintenance. Any fluctuations in the light source will create streaks in the captured image. Dirt on the lead screw that traverses the head will set up a pattern in the image, and dust on any optical device will reduce sharpness.

Drum scanners often use a Xenon light source to analyze the image. This extremely bright beam of perfectly white light can penetrate and extract detail from even the darkest of transparencies. If an image is underexposed or very dark, a drum scanner will capture more low light detail than can any of the flat bed or digital camera scanners.

Flat bed scanning

The difference between flat bed and drum scanning comes with the photo sensor. Drum scanners have one relatively large photo sensor that is used to analyze every pixel in the image. Flat bed scanners have arrays of tiny photo sensors arranged in a tight line, and each sensor records one pixel in a line of data.

Flat bed scanners operate on the same mechanical principles as a Xerox machine. The copy either passes over a linear array of photo sensors, or the array moves under the copy. Charged Coupled Devices (CCD) have been used in scanners for approximately eight years. Their development is highly scientific, and involves technologies at the most sophisticated level of today's sciences. The advantage of a flat bed scanner is its cost. With fewer mechanical and optical parts, flat bed CCD scanners can be relatively inexpensive. Their quality continues to improve, and with recent breakthroughs in CCD research, the quality of a flat bed CCD scanner matches the best drum scanners on most images.

Digital Cameras

Digital cameras are the most recent development in scanning technology. Instead of having only one line of photo sensors in an array, an entire matrix of photo sensors is arranged on a large-scale integrated circuit. This matrix array of photo sensors is used to replace the film in a normal single-lens reflex camera. The developments in this technology revolve around making higher resolution photo sensor arrays, and miniaturizing the design to fit in traditional camera equipment. The advantage of digital cameras is in speed and cost. The tradeoff today is in quality. Current technology limits professional-quality results to images smaller than eight by ten inches in size. Image content has a great deal to do with the acceptability of digital camera images today, but it won't be long before digital cameras are as common as traditional film cameras.

COLOR SPACE

There are a number of empirical ways to describe color, and each is referred to as color space. Color space is always described three-dimensionally. The simplest model is a cube. Each corner of the cube has a primary color assigned to it, and the opposite diagonal corners form the poles of the gray access. A color space in digital imaging defines all the reproducible colors available within the limitations of the process employed.

The additive colors, red, green, and blue, describe the range of colors that can be created by projecting beams of colored light onto a completely reflective surface. The substractive color space, CMY, describes a surface's ability to capture projected light and prevent it from being reflected. Television monitors work by projecting red, green, and blue beams of light. All computer-based imaging relies on the RGB color space to display the digital data.

The process of placing ink on paper works with the CMY color space. Black is added to help enhance detail, and it is necessary because of our limited ability to transfer large amounts of ink to paper, and the difficulty of manufacturing pure cyan, magenta, and yellow dyes.

Changing from one color space to another involves a translation process. This can change the integrity of an image. Do not change from RGB to CMYK colorspace unless you have tested the process thoroughly and know the translation results.

HUE SATURATION AND VALUE (HSV)

Another way to describe color is in terms of its hue, saturation, and value. There are a number of defined color spaces that use this method, and they have some definite advantages.

The Hue axes are orange, purple, lime, and anything else that is between two primary colors. The hue axis in the color space forms the outer surface. If you imagined an HSV color space as the globe, hue would reach its maximum values around the equator, and value would pass through the center of the earth to form the poles.

Saturation is determined by a hue's distance from the center polar axis. The more saturated a color is, the greater its purity, and the closer its "S" value is to the surface of the color space globe. As colors become less saturated, they appear duller, grayer. The least saturated colors are closest to the gray polar axis. These colors are more difficult to reproduce faithfully. Scanners are programmed to maintain gray balance, and colors that are almost gray can be affected by the "Gray Balance Window" of the scanner.

Gray balance is a term that defines the exact ratio of the cyan, magenta, and yellow printing inks that combine to create a perfectly neutral gray. A typical combination of mid-tone gray balance values is 65% Cyan, 53% Magenta, and 55% Yellow. Often the yellow and magenta are the same value, but in this case the example suggests that the contamination of magenta in yellow ink and vice versa is slightly different. Cyan ink is the least pure primary ink. Cyan has a quantity of magenta and yellow contamination in it. If equal amounts of the three inks are printed on paper, the result will be brown. To obtain a balanced gray, less magenta and yellow are needed because of their contaminating presence in the cyan ink.

A gray balance window defines the correct combination of a given set of inks necessary to reproduce a neutral gray scale, and establishes how near-neutral colors will be affected by this relationship. Scanners have a gray balance window built into them. Many are not adjustable. When evaluating a scanner's reproduction capabilities, use a color chart with a full range of near-neutral colors, and observe how the scanner takes a dark green or a near-neutral blue, and makes them neutral. If this sounds like a problem, it is. The solution lies in expertise.

COLOR CORRECTION

Color correction involves making adjustments to the captured color data in order to obtain a desired output. This is accomplished through the development of a lookup table. The lookup table reads data in, adjusts it, and writes new data out.

The simplest form of a lookup table is two dimensional. Given a value of X, adjust to a new value of $X+n$. Most black and white film recorders are calibrated using a two-dimensional lookup table. The problem with a two-dimensional lookup table approach to color correction is that it only considers adjustments to the primary components of the color space. Corrections are limited to very global moves. Complex colors such as those found in flesh tones cannot be isolated from reds and yellows.

Two-dimensional lookup tables have the advantage of being simple to calculate. This form of color correction and output calibration is widely employed in desktop computer software today. Macintosh programs such as Photoshop™ and ColorStudio™ offer two-dimensional curves with which to adjust color. These programs are not adequate to allow users to transform an RGB color space into CMYK with the level of quality necessary to equal the results of a high-end computer system.

This is a temporary problem that will be solved with faster hardware and better software. For now, professional-quality color separations can best be achieved by using high-quality color corrected scans already recorded in a thirty-two bit CMYK color space.

Only high-end systems and expensive output film recorders have three-dimensional color correction capability. Three-dimensional color correction calculates a lookup value for every color in the model. Most of today's systems can produce 16.7 million colors, and a three-dimensional lookup table can calculate a correction value for every one. This approach requires considerable computing power, and it yields very accurate results.

Color correction is a process of bending the color space to match a desired result as closely as possible. Blending is a delicate process that can cause banding, posterizing, and reversals if it is taken too far. Color correction can best be achieved using high end scanners. High-end scanners have been fitted with color computers that sample twelve bits per primary color. At this volume of data, correction is extremely precise and results can be very smooth. The scanner's computer resamples the corrected data to output an optimized eight bits per color.

Color correction is complicated, and it is difficult to write about it without employing very technical models and referring to mathematical algorithms that will not mean much to the artist who simply wants great color.

The best way to deal with color correction is through the test image. Record all the scanner settings so that the process can be repeated. Color correct using either the scanner controls or the application software. Only manipulate one variable at a time until you are confident of the results. Any time a new process is to be employed, test it first before live work is commited. Digital data is very precise. Once an image is altered, it can be impossible to reverse the process. If you are not sure, save the unaltered version.

OUTPUT DEVICES

There are a host of devices that have been developed to output color image data to hard copy. There are two primary categories of devices-film recorders and proofers. Film recorders process every line of digital data, and every byte per pixel. Film records either output each color on a separate piece of black and white film or expose all colors onto a single sheet of color-sensitive film.

The film recorder works by converting digital data into a modulating light source that exposes film. Film is exposed in one of two ways—either it is done line by line, or the whole picture is displayed on a TV tube and then a picture is taken of it. The picture-tube approach is less expensive. Color is achieved by displaying each color channel separately and in exact register. Filters are used to introduce the color needed to expose the different dye layers.

Picture tube film recorders are called CRT (Cathode Ray Tube) film recorders. The results from these devices can be very good, but they do not equal the precision imaging obtainable through film recorders that expose using a scanning beam. Scanning beam recorders expose film one pixel at a time. The cost and quality differences in these devices are dependent on the precision with which a pixel is exposed.

There are two ways of exposing film with a scanning beam. One way, Copstand recording, involves the precise movement of the film across a beam of modulating light. The other method, "Moving Beam," has two variations. One involves holding the film securely in place while a lead screw moves a scanning beam across the surface of the film. The other variation mimics the rotary drum scanner. Film is mounted on a spinning drum and a beam of light travels across the length of the spinning film, exposing it line by line.

The variables that determine the ultimate quality of any film recorder are the mechanical precision of the film exposure system and the accuracy with which the digital data is converted into modulating light. The latter is as important as the former. The digital data to be exposed may have a well-balanced thirty-two bit pixel, but unless the exposure system can faithfully translate the digital values to light on film the results will suffer.

For every film recorder on the market there is a patentable variation on the mechanical and optical engineering employed to expose the film. Film recorder prices are falling, and the quality of their output is improving. It is safe to say that the depreciation on a film recorder is very rapid, and one should plan for obsolescence in the short term.

Most film recorders are "dumb" devices. This means that they only expose film based on a signal that commands the expose modulator. The command signal originates from a Raster Image Processor (RIP). A RIP can exist either as software within a standard computer or as special purpose hardware. Most early RIPs were hardware-oriented because of the intensive calculations involved in processing the raster signal, and the need for speed.

Microprocessor and software technology have advanced considerably, so many of the newer RIPs utilize standard microcomputer hardware and involve very sophisticated software.

A Postscript RIP is programmed to accept the Postscript Page Description Language, and it converts the contents of the Postscript document to a bit map that can be exposed line by line using a film recorder. The lines of data to be exposed are called Raster Lines. A discussion of Postscript would be too verbose for this chapter, but, simply stated, Postscript is a computer language developed by Adobe Systems, Inc. that is structured to describe all of the elements on a page, and their relationship to each other and to the page.

DOT GENERATION, SCREEN RULINGS, AND ANGLES

Halftone printing is the most popular method of reproducing photographic images with ink on paper. The process involves fooling the eye by taking advantage of an optical system. The eye cannot resolve very small dots that are placed very close together. When the frequency of dots making up a pattern is increased to approximately 150 within a single inch, the dots appear to form a continuous straight line. It takes a magnifying glass to reveal that the line is composed of a string of tiny dots.

An offset printing press transfers ink from a printing plate to a rubber blanket, which in turn transfers the ink to paper. The press does not allow for local variations in the quantity of ink that is transferred. Therefore, a continuous tone image, exposed to a lithographic printing plate, is very difficult to resolve as ink on paper. There are specialty reproduction printers who have developed a method of offset continuous tone printing, but this process is extremely difficult to control, works for very limited quantities, and is limited to the art reproduction market.

THE NEW FRONTIER

Input, output, and quality control procedures will continue to evolve and improve. New systems designed to improve calibration are already on the market. EFI color, a software calibration system developed by EFI (Electronics For Imaging), is being bundled with Quark Express software. The system helps artists obtain more accurate color on their monitors, proofs, and final output.

EFI color is not the panacea of calibration and color quality control, but it is the first of many products to come that will improve quality control. Ultimately, all the hardware and software tools neccessary to perform the highest quality color work possible will be available for an artist to call upon. Then it will come back to the artist, who will still have to have the talent, discipline, and motivation to produce a quality product.

The new frontier for desktop publishing lies in alternative media, multi-media, and interactive media. The once separate disciplines of print, television, video, and audio are rapidly converging to create new creative opportunities. Artists must learn to see beyond the blur of technology in order to focus on real needs and tangible results. Technology certainly makes it much easier to produce mediocre art. It has also increased the possibilities for new art, and, when applied creatively, will raise the overall "State of the Art."

The images used in this chapter: Input, Output, and Quality Control are taken from two AGFA publications, *An Introduction to Digital Color Prepress*, and *Digital Color Prepress—Volume Two*. For information on purchasing these useful reference books, contact Agfa at (800) 395-7007.

Innovative Design Approaches

Perhaps the most radical departure taken from traditional assumptions about painting in this century arose directly out of the technology of reproduction. Unlike a paper collage, where one might tear images from newspapers and magazines to create a picture, artists are now trying to balance a multitude of computer cutouts with different levels of transparency. These images consist of photographic likenessess, real objects, and passages that have been created with a computer system, all united in a single dimension.

In this chapter there are thirty-one examples of digital photo illustration created specifically to examine the imaging possibilities available on most systems and software configurations today. This chapter also examines how the agency, separator, and printer function together, and it looks at production tips including suggestions for photography and 3D for print. Finally, there is the all-important issue of health and safety.

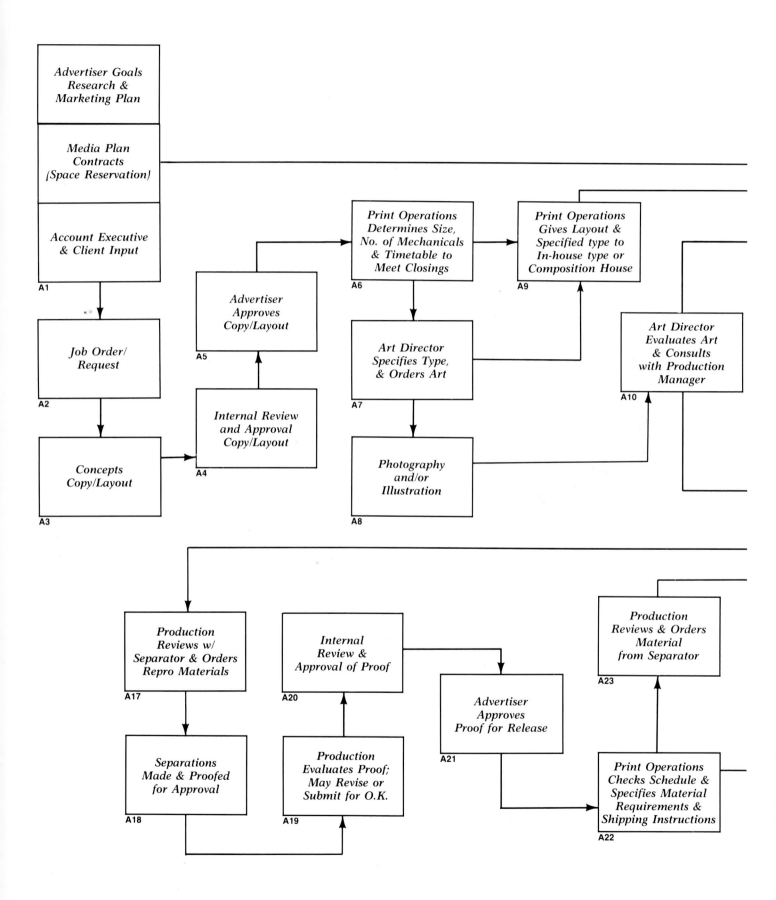

Advertiser Goals Research & Marketing Plan

Media Plan Contracts (Space Reservation)

Account Executive & Client Input
A1

Job Order/ Request
A2

Concepts Copy/Layout
A3

Internal Review and Approval Copy/Layout
A4

Advertiser Approves Copy/Layout
A5

Print Operations Determines Size, No. of Mechanicals & Timetable to Meet Closings
A6

Art Director Specifies Type, & Orders Art
A7

Photography and/or Illustration
A8

Print Operations Gives Layout & Specified type to In-house type or Composition House
A9

Art Director Evaluates Art & Consults with Production Manager
A10

Production Reviews w/ Separator & Orders Repro Materials
A17

Separations Made & Proofed for Approval
A18

Internal Review & Approval of Proof
A20

Production Evaluates Proof; May Revise or Submit for O.K.
A19

Advertiser Approves Proof for Release
A21

Print Operations Checks Schedule & Specifies Material Requirements & Shipping Instructions
A22

Production Reviews & Orders Material from Separator
A23

The Agency

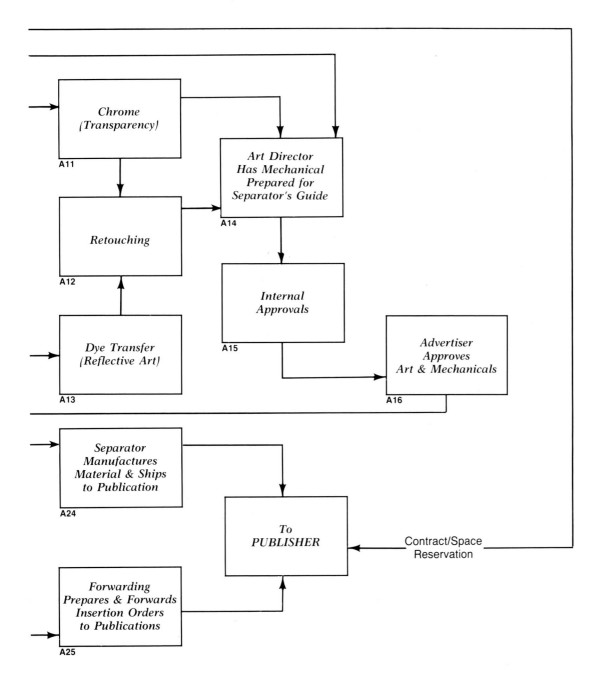

Reprinted with permission from the Graphic Communications Association
(GCA). This chart is excerpted from GCA's *Measure 21 Process Guide.* To
order the complete booklet, contact GCA at 100 Daingerfield Road,
Alexandria, VA 22314; (703) 519-8160

The Separator

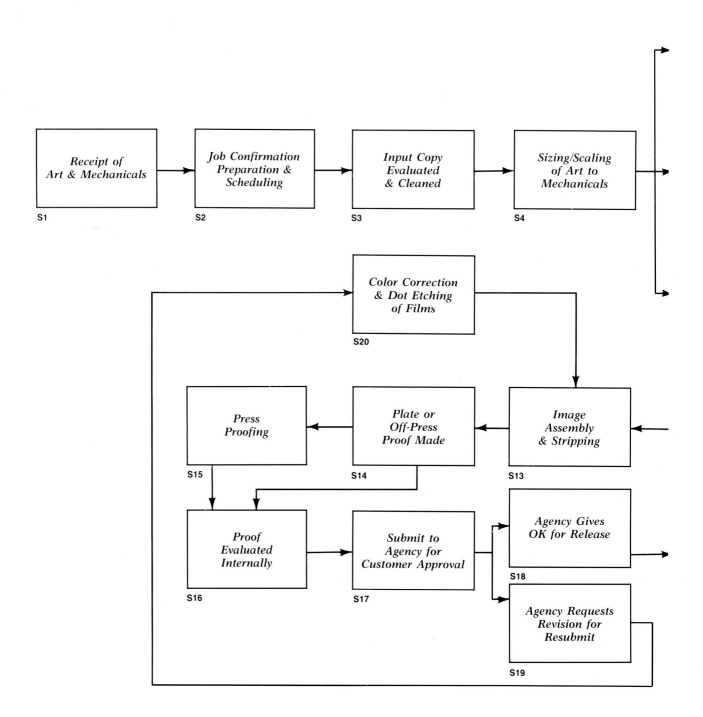

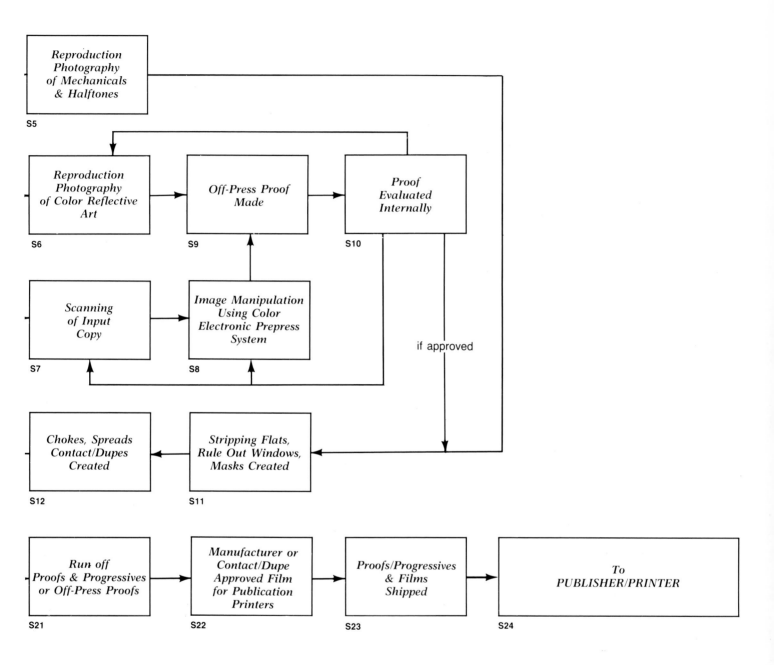

Reproduction Photography of Mechanicals & Halftones — S5

Reproduction Photography of Color Reflective Art — S6

Off-Press Proof Made — S9

Proof Evaluated Internally — S10

Scanning of Input Copy — S7

Image Manipulation Using Color Electronic Prepress System — S8

if approved

Chokes, Spreads Contact/Dupes Created — S12

Stripping Flats, Rule Out Windows, Masks Created — S11

Run off Proofs & Progressives or Off-Press Proofs — S21

Manufacturer or Contact/Dupe Approved Film for Publication Printers — S22

Proofs/Progressives & Films Shipped — S23

To PUBLISHER/PRINTER — S24

Reprinted with permission from the Graphic Communications Association (GCA). This chart is excerpted from GCA's *Measure 21 Process Guide*. To order the complete booklet, contact GCA at 100 Daingerfield Road, Alexandria, VA 22314; (703) 519-8160

The Printer

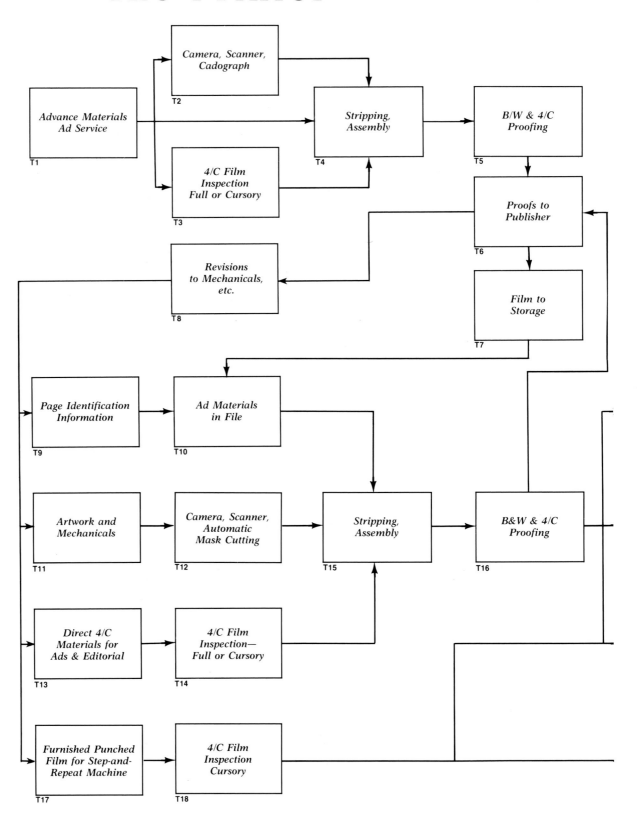

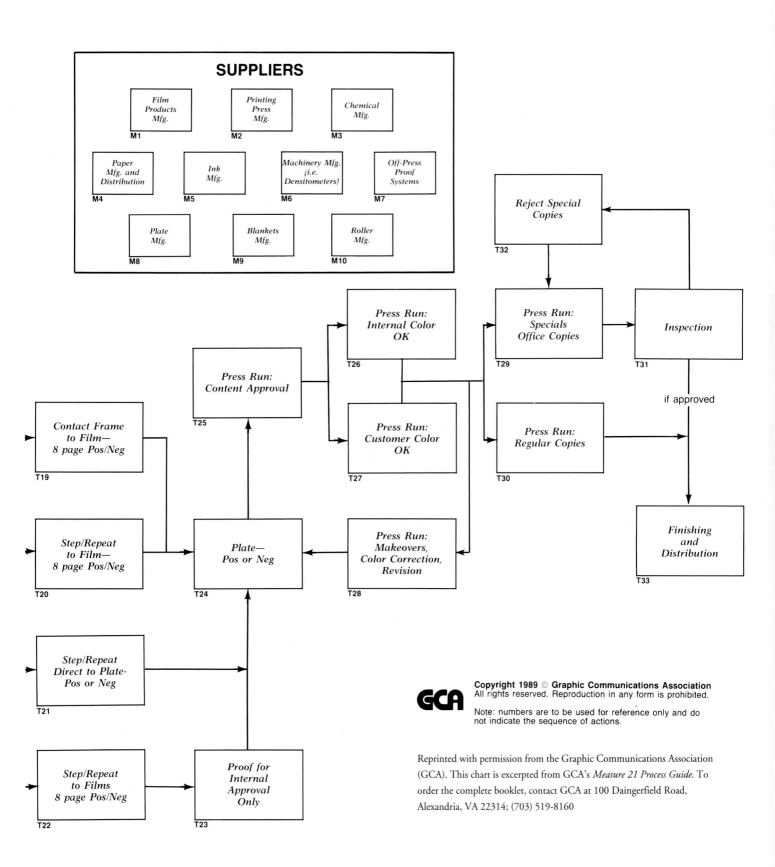

SUPPLIERS

Film Products Mfg. M1	*Printing Press Mfg.* M2	*Chemical Mfg.* M3

Paper Mfg. and Distribution M4	*Ink Mfg.* M5	*Machinery Mfg. (i.e. Densitometers)* M6	*Off-Press Proof Systems* M7

Plate Mfg. M8	*Blankets Mfg.* M9	*Roller Mfg.* M10

Reject Special Copies T32

Press Run: Internal Color OK T26

Press Run: Content Approval T25

Contact Frame to Film— 8 page Pos/Neg T19

Press Run: Customer Color OK T27

Press Run: Specials Office Copies T29

Inspection T31

if approved

Press Run: Regular Copies T30

Step/Repeat to Film— 8 page Pos/Neg T20

Plate— Pos or Neg T24

Press Run: Makeovers, Color Correction, Revision T28

Finishing and Distribution T33

Step/Repeat Direct to Plate- Pos or Neg T21

Step/Repeat to Films 8 page Pos/Neg T22

Proof for Internal Approval Only T23

Reprinted with permission from the Graphic Communications Association (GCA). This chart is excerpted from GCA's *Measure 21 Process Guide.* To order the complete booklet, contact GCA at 100 Daingerfield Road, Alexandria, VA 22314; (703) 519-8160

At any moment in time a designer deals with a variety of very difficult jobs, all in various stages of completion. Design and production is difficult to automate for this very reason. It is not a simple linear process as the previous flow diagrams illustrate.

PHOTOGRAPHY

Photographic techniques have given advertising a new look each decade. Clients today have visual ideas that are influenced by computer effects they have seen in video and film.

Artists, designers, and photographers need help to create images that will make the most of a complex production path of digital and film-based steps. They should not waste time on aspects of a shoot that can be better handled by the computer. The operator should also suggest ways to set up the photograph for the maximum ease in final compositing. Understanding what will happen to the image in the computer also affects the way the photographer decides how to shoot the initial image.

If you are not taking the photographs yourself, make sure that you have a reliable photographer. But be sure you give him or her all the facts about the project so it can be shot with your final image in mind. Ask the photographer to shoot backup material so elements can be taken from it if necessary. Are you shooting all your elements for your digital photo composition with uniform lighting? Do you need a special effect created in the camera? Make sure your composition, picture elements, lighting, and subject are all explained at the start. Make sure your photographer understands print. He or she can adjust the shooting accordingly by adapting lighting ratios to your printing needs.

Knowing your photography is only one step on the way to your completed digital photo illustration. It should affect the way you think about the shoot. It is much better to shoot specific photographs to fit an intended design. Help the photographer avoid wasting time on aspects of the shoot that can be done easily on the computer. Make sure the photographer takes the photograph for maximum ease in final compositing. Photograph the separate parts carefully, bearing in mind the lighting and perspective—although both can be corrected later, such

corrections will be more time-consuming and costly. The only limitations will be
your imagination and the photography you have to work with.

Make sure that you are always working with the original, not with a
composite chrome or a composite print that has been hand-retouched. Although
your chrome may be only a part of your final digital photo illustration, and it can
have many adjustments made to it, do not rely on the computer to clean up
mistakes that could have been avoided during the shoot. These changes will cost
you time and money. Never touch chromes that are to be scanned. Always keep
them in plastic sleeves, and avoid paper clips. Markups and instructions can be
drawn on color prints rather than on film sleeves, as sometimes the instructions
are removed by accident.

Use a low emulsion speed that will still give you the results you need for the
photograph. A low emulsion speed will give you a long tonal scale and saturated
color, and it will have almost no grain. Choose one film type and become familiar
with its qualities. Never mix large format and 35mm stock scans in a composition,
because one will be sharper than the other and that will affect the realism.

Lighting is very important in taking the photographs you need for your
project. Experiment with your lighting, try all the variations, take lots of
exposures, and bracket. Make sure that there is light in your shadow areas to pick
up details for your chromes.

When we perceive the world through our eyes, we experience it through the
full range of visible color. When we take a photograph and use, for example,
transparency film, the range of color is limited to what is possible with that
medium. No single medium has the same color bandwidth as the human eye.
How we observe color is the key to understanding the transfer of color between
red, green, and blue on a computer screen and the print color space of cyan,
magenta, yellow, and black. This creates a difficult situation in which to reproduce
images in print, and this is why the conversion of RGB images to the color space
of CMYK is a complex process. Separations are key to the quality of a printed
piece and quality control at this point will help with the successful translation of
color to an image in print.

If you output ten transparencies of the same image, this will ensure that
everyone, including the printer, the client, and the agency, get the same

information, although most clients would spend less if they had separations made instead. However, in the near future a global marketplace will require distribution of images in a digital form.

When you cannot get the shot you need or your budget does not allow for a location shoot, consider the world of stock. Because many agencies carry a large variety of images, the chances are that you will find exactly what you are looking for. Always talk to a researcher, since you can always get advice if you are not exactly sure of what you want. Stock agencies will make every effort to find exactly what you need. Always make sure that the rights have been cleared for use. Also remember there is never a standard fee. Charges are based on usage. Using stock may be the solution to finding and securing the image you want to finish your assignment.

3D FOR PRINT

It is possible to take advantage of the qualities that computers create for animation, but why not use them instead for still images in print applications? For example, using a 3D model allows the artist to dictate all the color changes and lighting of an object, as well as to decide on camera angles and perspective views that would be time-consuming if made with a paint program. When you create your own model you own the copyright, and you have complete control if the object you want to use is difficult to find or photograph.

By using procedural texture maps, different looks for objects can be created easily. Because they are based on algorithms, the textures can be created at different print quality resolutions. This would not be possible if the textures were scanned or made with a paint program.

HEALTH AND SAFETY

More than 3000 research papers have been written on VDU terminal sickness. There are major hazards—radiation and the problems that result from bad posture. Related illness can surface in the form of back problems, eye strain, and frequent headaches.

Eye-related problems are common because the light produced by a VDU is unsuitable for human eye and brain patterns. You should be able to control screen brightness and contrast, cut down on glare, and have the screen fitted with an earthed antistatic device. Screens should be switched off to minimize radiation effects when they are not being used. If you are close to a monitor while you work, you are being exposed to an electromagnetic field. These fields have electrical and magnetic components. Electromagnetic energy can be VLF (Very Low Frequency) and ELF (Extremely Low Frequency) radiation. ELF is the most dangerous. However, any magnetic component of electromagnetic radiation is unhealthy. Although companies that make computers make no mention of health risks, some now have to deal with standards being introduced by health and safety councils outside the United States, standards that require more stringent control of electromagnetic emission controls. Already there are companies that will conduct environmental tests in the workplace. Some tips they offer to reduce health risks include turning off all electrical equipment when it is not in use and staying at least two feet from your monitor (radiation recedes with distance). Check the positions of computers in other rooms nearby, since you can be effected by a machine you cannot see—solid walls do not keep electromagnetic fields out! Do not use materials in the workplace that can create electrostatic fields—for example, stay away from plastics in such things as carpeting and curtains. Always keep the workplace well aired, and use a magnetic shield around the back of the cathode ray tube.

To reduce static, wear natural fibers, and have an antistatic desk mat and floor mat, and use a dust cover for the screen. A VDU attracts dust when it is on—combine this with static and positive ions and you end up with blocked pores, dry skin, and sore eyes. A personal ioniser on the desktop counters the static produced by a VDU, which empties the air of negative ions and so leaves too many damaging positive ions in the air. Plants are good to have around as they keep the air clean. Spider plants will soak up any extra carbon monoxide.

Back problems can be reduced by ergonomic chairs. You should always sit erect with good lumbar support. At least once an hour, stand up and do some pelvic tilts to reduce the pressure on the discs in your lower back. Keep the pressure from the seat of the chair off your thighs, as this can press on the sciatic nerve.

Repetitive strain injury (RSI) begins with strain on the back, shoulders, neck, hands, and wrists from performing the same movements continuously. While manual typewriters required movement from the whole arm, to use a computer an operator works with only fingers on the keyboard, sometimes sitting in a bad position for hours on end. As early as 1964 Japan recognized RSI illness, and laid down stringent regulations for computer operators, but today operators in Japan, Europe, Australia, and the United States are still being afflicted. Today it is important to be aware of RSI, and to take steps to counteract the strain of awkward posture, and to place importance on office ergonomics.

Other health factors associated with computers are increasingly being unearthed. Therefore, the message is be aware of these discoveries and protect yourself accordingly.

Adjustable
screen

Good lighting

15°

Balanced head
position

Shoulders relaxed

Clothes
made of
natural
fibers

Upper arm vertical

Adjustable screen
and stand

Static
wrist position

Forearms horizontal

Personal ioniser

lower lumbar
region

Flat keyboard

Adjustable
backrest

Thin desk top
for maximum
thigh space

Anti static mat

Adjustable chair

Moveable
stable base

Feet flat on floor
or footrest

Plants to reduce
carbon monoxide

Amporn Klatray

50/50

This image of a still life bridges the gap between illustration and photography. It is fifty percent photograph and fifty percent illustration. The elements were carefully arranged by cutting and pasting and then some areas were rendered using the drawing and painting tools in the paint program. A lattice work of finely drawn lines imitate what could be the drawing of a Rennaisance master. (Image: Charissa Baker)

Fig. 1 – 1. *A still life of a pomegranate, leaves, and a snail is photographed in the studio. This photograph is the basis for the final composition.*

Fig. 1 – 2. *This studio photograph of berries is used as a basis for electronic sgraffito, a technique that uses a layer of photographic information as a guideline for another drawn or painted layer. (In this instance, a pencil drawing.) If an attempt is unsuccessful, the photographic layer is restored and the process begins again. This may continue until a satisfactory result is achieved.*

Fig. 1 – 3. *Various hazelnuts and walnuts are extracted from this studio photograph and used in the final composition. Sgraffito is used on some of the nuts in the final composition.*

Fig. 1 – 4. *Both flesh and seeds are used for details in the final pomegranate composite.*

Fig. 1 – 6. *The background stencil is used as the underlying pattern for a variegated wash. This is accomplished using electronic frottage. The stencil is drawn through numerous times until the density and texture the background stencil produces creates a satisfactory graded tone.*

Fig. 1 – 5. *Stencil of pomegranate to protect foreground from electronic frottage used in the background.*

HOT ROD

Almost every automobile advertisement placed by a top agency in a national circulation magazine has been retouched. In this image something has been created out of nothing. A hot rod has been made from a family sedan through the use of image-enhancing techniques. Enhancement is more painterly, more the artist's tool. In the final image a textile design is scanned and used for the customized paintwork. (Image: Rory Baxter)

Fig. 2 – 1. *Sketch of imaginary hot rod.*

Fig. 2 – 2. *Original family sedan*

Fig. 2 – 3. *Windows and interior squashed down for aerodynamic effect.*

Fig. 2 – 5. *Detailing and customizing with electronic airbrushing.*

Fig. 2 – 4. *Bodywork redesigned wider tires and wheel arches.*

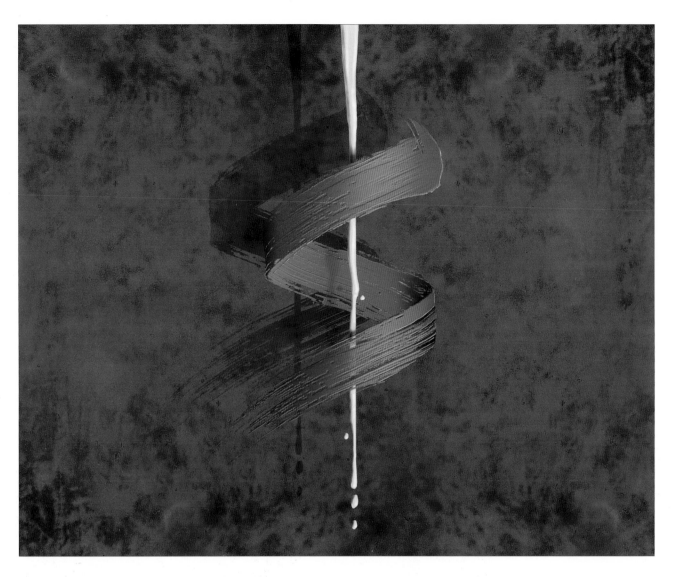

BRUSHSTROKE

This image of intertwined brush strokes was rendered with scanned imagery and textures. Paint textures were then embossed onto the final form to add to the illusion of 3D calligraphy. (Image: Rory Baxter)

Fig. 3 – 1. *Using a textured image synthesis program, a concrete colored backdrop was created for a background.*

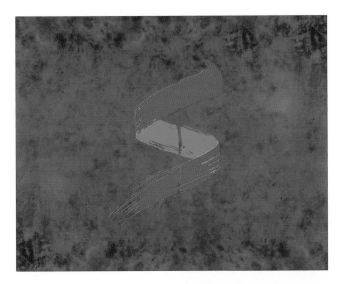

Fig. 3 – 2. *A medium such as tempera or acrylic was used to create a selection of brushstrokes on paper. These strokes were then scanned and assembled into a spiral.*

Fig. 3 – 3. *The drip was initially created by pouring ink onto paper. This created some extraordinary and unpredictable effects. The drip was colorized and retouched to create a volumetric effect.*

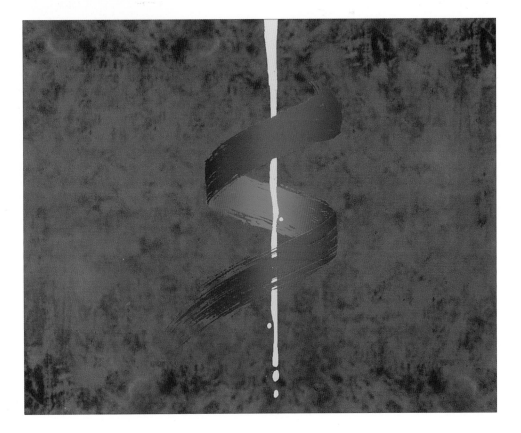

EARTH DICE

*This unusual view of two dice is a mixture of 3D modelling, an oil painting of
the earth, and a star field created photographically. All the elements were
composited, retouched, and color corrected, and the glow was added using a paint
system. (Image: Robert Bowen. R/Greenberg Associates, Inc.)*

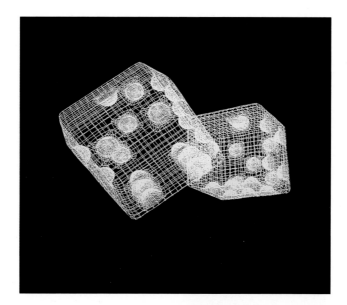

Fig. 4 – 1. *Substractive Boolean spheres were imbedded in the wire frame cubes. The edges were softened.*

Fig. 4 – 2. *An oil painting of the earth was made and digitized. The data was then mapped on the wire frame dice model. Two different lighting characteristics were used. The water was given shiny attributes and the land masses assigned nonreflecting attributes.*

Fig. 4 – 3. *Procedural turbulence was used for the initial background.*

Fig. 4 – 4. *The star field was created optically with a 2D paint system.*

TEXTURE WRAP

*The famous fur-covered cup, saucer, and spoon by Meret Oppenheim in the
collection of the Museum of Modern Art in New York was the initial inspiration
for this chair wrapped in spaghetti. The outlines of the chair are reinforced with
shading and highlights appropriate to the original lighting of the chair in the
studio. (Image: Terri Finnin Hunt. Printbox)*

Fig. 5 – 1. *An old high-backed chair is photographed as the armature for a metamorphosis.*

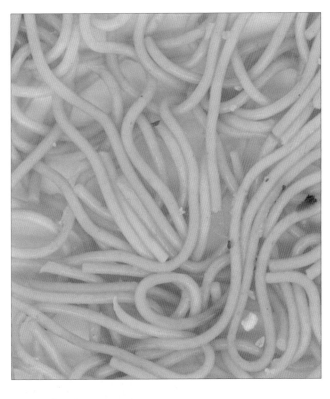

Fig. 5 – 2. *Spaghetti is then scanned on the flat bed scanner.*

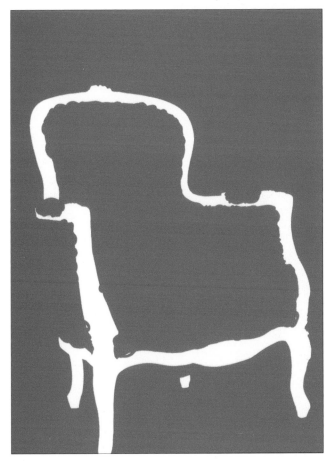

Fig. 5 – 3. *Stencils are created to protect the chair's wooden- framed upholstery sections.*

Fig. 5 – 5. *Spaghetti forms are then pasted into the upholstery stencil.*

Fig. 5 – 4. *More stencils are created to protect the upholstery stencil.*

Fig. 6 – 1. *Photograph of grapes.*

Fig. 6 – 2. *Initial sketch of grapes.*

Fig. 6 – 4. *Filter effect.*

Fig. 6 – 5. *Filter effect.*

Fig. 6 – 3. *Sensitive shading and continuous tones were used to define this pencil sketch.*

Fig. 6 – 6. *The rich tones of a charcoal drawing emphasize the tonal rather than the linear qualities in this drawing.*

GRAPES

Oil paint, pencil, charcoal, and chalk are now recreated as digital painting media in a paint program. High resolution monitors allow individual brushstrokes to break through and allow a gesture to be captured in a matrix of pixels. Filters can be used to create complex spatial arrangements and interlocking planes of transparent color. (Image: Alex Fraytor)

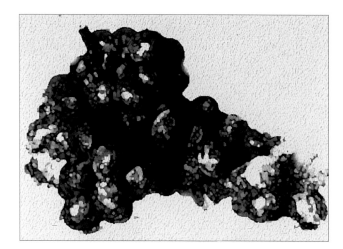

Fig. 6 – 7. *A graphite and water mix create another monochromatic study.*

Fig. 6 – 9. *Marker drawing.*

Fig. 6 – 10. *Oil painting on rough ground.*

Fig. 6 – 8. *Pastel drawing.*

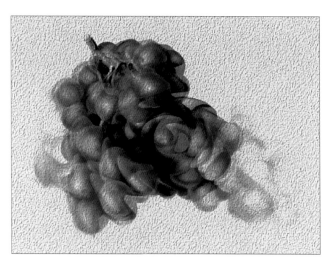

Fig. 6 – 12. *Filter effect.*

Fig. 6 – 11. *Filter effect.*

7 – 1. *Spring.*

7 – 4. *Fall.*

7 – 2. *Winter.*

LANDSCAPES

Long before anyone dreamt of satellite pictures or holiday snaps, artists were making images of the landscape. The intention of these images of the seasons is to strip away all the scene-setting representational elements of a landscape, and play along the shifting blurred boundary between abstraction and figuration— creating a textural abstract image about the experience *of landscape, not just its appearance. The random placement of texture-mapped 3D objects camouflaged by the use of filters on selected areas gives a painterly quality to each of these images. (Image: Alex Fraytor. Speed Graphics)*

7 – 3. *Summer.*

PRISONER

Inspired by Michelangelo's sculptures of slaves, this image of a partially finished stone statue comes to life through a combination of electronic retouching and tinting. (Image: Paul French. Saffron Studio)

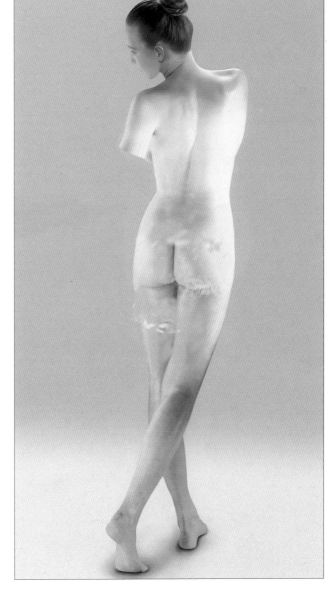

Fig. 8 – 2. *The model is tinted to resemble stone. The ear is redrawn where it is obscured by the phone, the arm is severed to emphasize the feel of a Greek statue. A background is created from "noise."*

Fig. 8 – 1. *Model photographed in a studio setting.*

Fig. 8 – 3. *The base of the statue is created from a photograph of plaster. Perspective distortion is then used to create a solid block.*

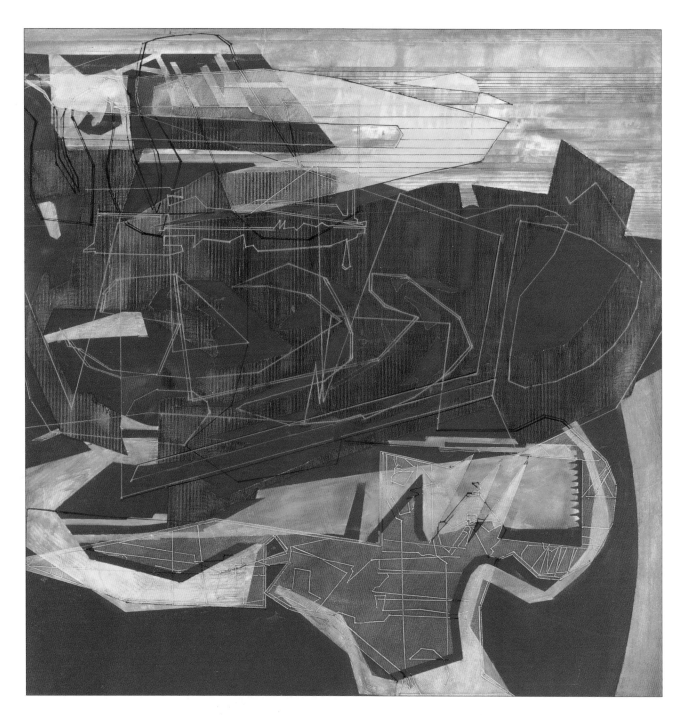

COAST OF AFRICA

This abstract landscape is based on the pictorial language of the computer, embracing both vector and raster graphics. Traditional and digital media are used at the input and output stages, creating an unusual contrast of mediums. The visual fundamentals emphasized by the cubists were based mainly on contrasts. Other contrasts employed in the image include dark and light, positive and negative, perforated and solid, curved and straight.
(Image: Jeremy Gardiner)

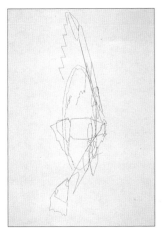
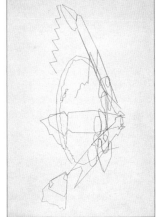

Fig. 9 – 1. *Vector plot.*   **Fig. 9 – 2.** *Vector plot.*

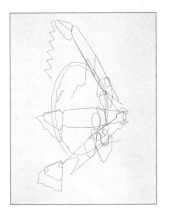
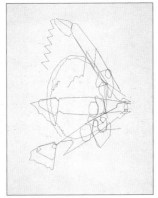
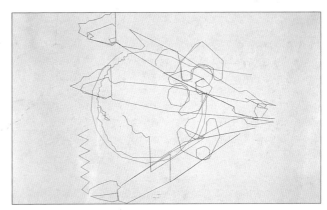

Fig. 9 – 3. *Vector plot.*   **Fig. 9 – 4.** *Vector plot.*   **Fig. 9 – 5.** *Vector plot.*

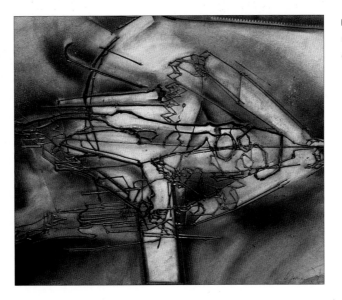

Fig. 9 – 6. *A drawing based on the vector plots is made with graphite on paper.*

TELEGENIC CHARISMA

An enormous number of television images are close-ups of faces. A face in close-up is the sharpest signal that television can produce while still conveying content. "Pontiff" is a television evangelist from this world of synthesized seamless characters. The final image is projected on canvas and painted with stencils to imitate the language of transmitted light seen on the screen.
(Image: Jeremy Gardiner)

Fig. 10 – 1. *A portrait is colorized and combined with an image of a keyhole.*

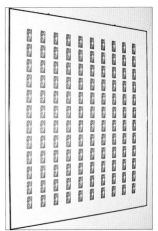

Fig. 10 – 2. *The portrait is stretched in a horizontal direction.*

Fig. 10 – 3. *The portrait is stretched in a vertical direction.*

Fig. 10 – 4. *A step-and-repeat ink jet print is made of the image.*

Fig. 10 – 5. *A large-scale thermal mosaic print is made as a cartoon for the final illustration.*

Fig. 10 – 6. *The cartoon alongside the final portrait on canvas.*

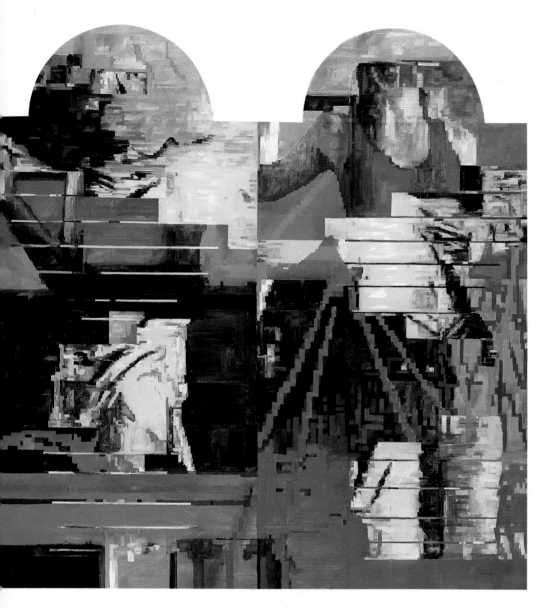

EXQUISITE CORPSE

The surrealists used to draw one part of a figure, fold the paper, thus hiding what they had drawn, and pass it on to the next member. The final composite figure, an "exquisite corpse," was revealed when the paper was unfolded. Like the Surrealist's exquisite corpse, television is about juxtaposition. An image of a girl is immediately adjacent with, perhaps, an image of the winged Victory of Samothrace. These juxtapositions are the cells of television's exquisite corpse. Using a filter to cut and splice these figures together illustrates the way a digital computer can cut an organic whole into inorganic parts and shuffle them around at megahertz speeds. As the power of resolution was adjusted up and down on the computer during the working process, the subjects became fields of multicolored squares that would await resolution in order to achieve comprehensibility. (Image: Jeremy Gardiner)

Fig. 11 – 1. *The Winged Victory of Samothrace from the Louvre.*

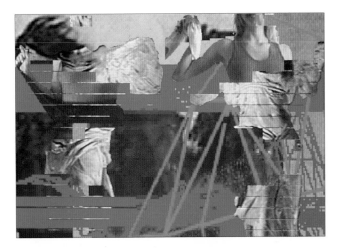

Fig. 11 – 3. *Cutout on blue background.*

Fig. 11 – 2. *The image of Victory and the model are then spliced together with green background.*

Fig. 11 – 4. *Figure cut into diptych with lunette to emphasize the head.*

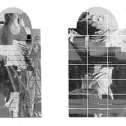

Fig. 11 – 5. *Divisions for output to thermal proof.*

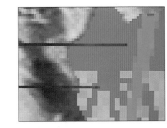

Fig. 11 – 6. *Single thermal proof.*

Fig. 11 – 7. *The large scale thermal proof is used as a guide for the final illustration.*

Fig. 12 – 2. *The atmospheric naturalism of the background is contrasted with the abstacted forms focused in the foreground.*

Fig. 12 – 1. *Photograph of the view from the balcony.*

Fig. 12 – 3. *Clone.*

Fig. 12 – 4. *Clone.*

BALLARD DOWN

The sensation of being in a particular landscape can best be conveyed not by imitating in paint the appearance of the landscape's parts, but by summoning up its essential nature through the use of light, space, and color. This view from a balcony uses image-processing techniques as a means of scrutinizing one location to create a series of images with different aesthetic and formal solutions. (Image: Jeremy Gardiner)

Fig. 12 – 5. *Clone.*

Fig. 12 – 6. *Clone.*

Fig. 12 – 7. *Clone.*

Fig. 12 – 8. *Clone.*

Fig. 12 – 9. *Clone.*

Fig. 12 – 10. *Clone.*

Fig. 12 – 11. *Clone.*

Fig. 12 – 13. *Clone.*

Fig. 12 – 12. *Clone.*

Fig. 12 – 14. *Clone.*

Fig. 13 – 1. *Stock photograph of a golden beach, blue water, and distant vista.*

A BIRD IN THE HAND

Salvador Dali's painting technique required photographic illusionism to challenge conventional ideas about reality. He called his pictures "handmade photographs." Much digital photo illustration owes a debt to Dali's imaginative and mysterious landscapes. Combining a plaster model of a hand, a stock shot, and an illustration of a bird goes some of the way towards emulating the surrealist quality of his work. (Image: Jeremy Gardiner)

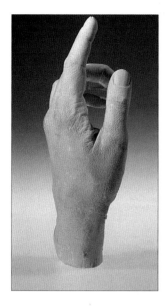

Fig. 13 – 2. *A plaster model of a hand is cast and then photographed in side elevation.*

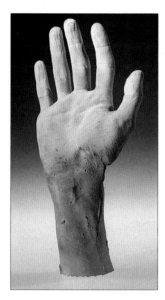

Fig. 13 – 3. *The plaster model of a hand is photographed in front elevation.*

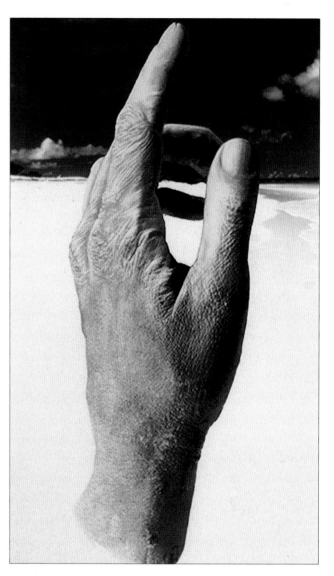

Fig. 13 – 6. *Reillustrated details of skin and wrinkles.*

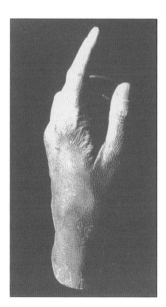

Fig. 13 – 4. *Stencil of hand.*

Fig. 13 – 5. *A white wash is made through the stencil to emphasize the stonelike quality of a monument.*

Fig. 13 – 7. *Bird illustration.*

Fig. 14 – 1a.

Fig. 14 – 1b.

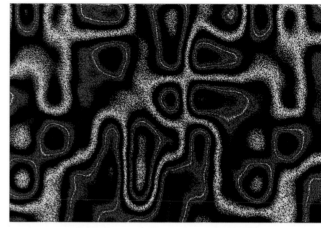

Fig. 14 – 1c.

Fig. 14 – 2a.

Fig. 14 – 2b.

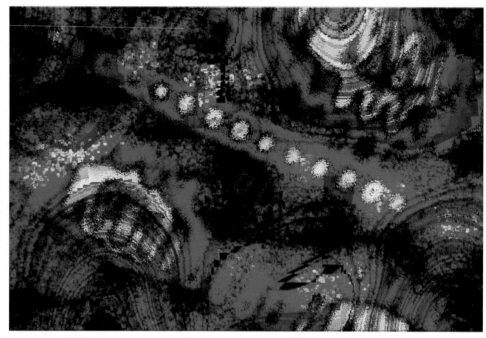

Fig. 14 – 2c.

ALGORITHMIC AESTHETIC

*Creating a series of abstract images using filters is a valid exercise but one that
relies heavily on the hidden point of view of the software. As Michel Foucault
points out, the more constrained we are by the choice of our actions the more
predictable the result will be. (Image: Jeremy Gardiner)*

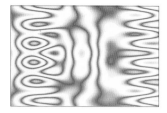

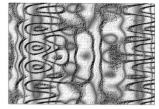

Fig. 14 – 3a.

Fig. 14 – 3b.

Fig. 14 – 3c.

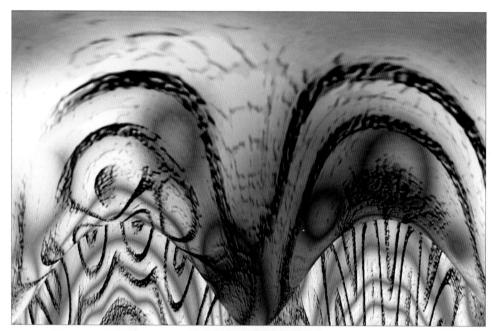

Fig. 14 – 4a.

Fig. 14 – 4b.

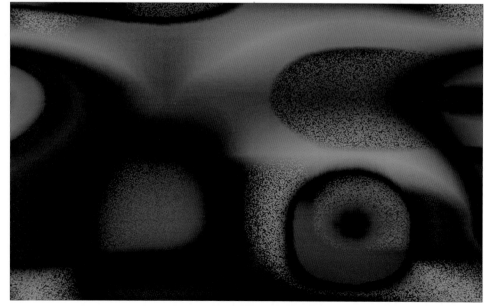

Fig. 14 – 4c.

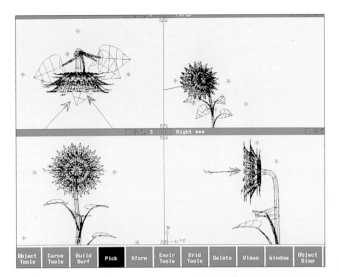
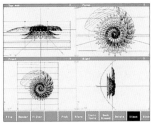
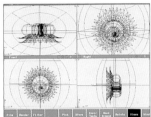

| Object Tools | Curve Tools | Build Surf | Pick | Xform | Envir Tools | Grid Tools | Delete | Views | Window | Object Disp |

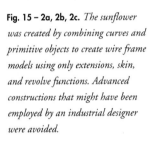

Fig. 15 – 2a, 2b, 2c. *The sunflower was created by combining curves and primitive objects to create wire frame models using only extensions, skin, and revolve functions. Advanced constructions that might have been employed by an industrial designer were avoided.*

Fig. 15 – 1. *Sunflower*
(© Mary Lowenbach)

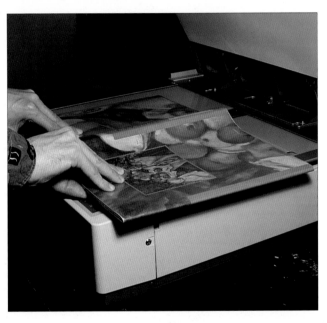

Fig. 15 – 3. *Textures were scanned and retouched before being used for bump, transparency, and reflection mapping onto the wire frame object.*

SUNFLOWER

During the Renaissance artists illustrated books and began to depict the plant world with increasing realism for naturalistic, decorative and symbolic purposes. By the end of the fifteenth century, we began seeing the earliest examples of Flemish and Dutch easel paintings using bouquets of flowers. Botanical art declined in the early twentieth century because flowers were being reproduced photographically. The camera provided the artist with close-ups and soft focus. Van Gogh was fascinated by the shape and color of sunflowers because they reminded him of fire, and in these studies a raycast technique reflects that characteristic.

Fig. 15 – 4. *Only two lights were assigned to the image and then executed simply.*

Fig. 15 – 5. *These strong intense lights were used to enhance the color value and texture of the image.*

Fig. 15 – 6. *A raycast rendering technique was used for the final rendering.*

Fig. 15 – 7. *In the final image the sunflower is combined with a model of a nautilus shell.*

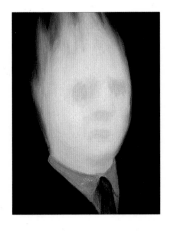

Fig. 16 – 1. *Initial illustration.*

Fig. 16 – 2. *Model photographed in suit and tie against black background to accentuate head and hands.*

Fig. 16 – 3. *The hand holding the cigarette is photographed separately for the final composition.*

Fig. 16 – 4. *Image of fire.*

Fig. 16 – 5. *Flames are cloned from the image of fire and then arranged to create a sense of volume similar to the original head and hands.*

FIREMAN

The use of transparent and translucent color glow through this fiery photo illustration. The irony of the unlit cigarette and the flame-broiled figure create an atmosphere of mystery much like the portraits of Rene Magritte.
(Image: Michael Kerbow. Printbox)

PUNK ROCK

Through electronic retouching, any image that an art director imagines can be created for the printed page. The most improbable changes, like these additions to Mount Rushmore, can look as natural as real life. In contrast to complex conventional techniques, which could well involve chemicals and darkroom tools, this digital photo illustration has been made with a series of digital manipulations to create a whimsical national monument. Most of the manipulation was accomplished by shifting picture information to retain the integrity of the rock texture. (Image: Michael Kerbow. Printbox)

Fig. 17 – 1. *Stock photograph of Mount Rushmore.*

RACIAL CHANGE

*Careful assembly, resizing, color correction, and illustration all go towards
making this portrait cross racial boundaries. A convincing likeness may fail to
present the spectator with the essential features of the person represented. Success
in making these images convincing lies in the reconstruction of the eyes, mouth
nose, and skin tones. (Image: Michael Kerbow. Printbox)*

Fig. 18 – 1. *Studio photograph of model.*

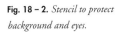

Fig. 18 – 2. *Stencil to protect background and eyes.*

Fig. 18 – 3. *Stencil to protect face.*

Fig. 18 – 4. *Blemishes removed, color of eyes and hair changed, earrings added.*

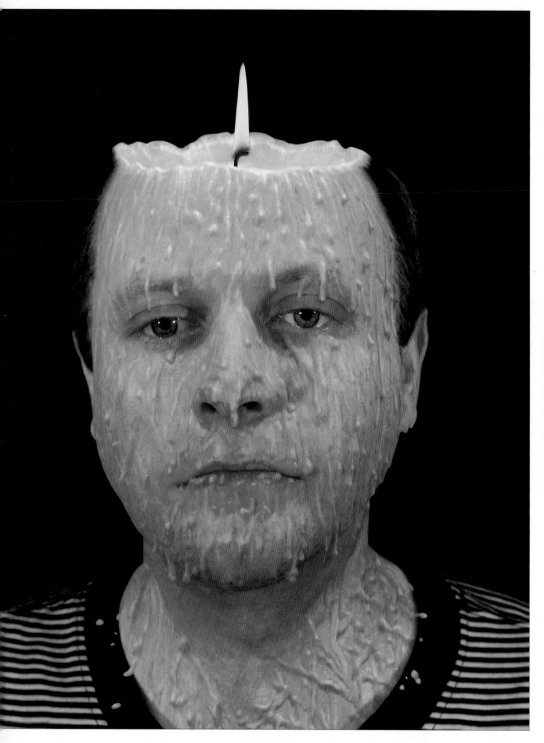

Fig. 19 – 1. *Original illustration.*

MELTDOWN

Liquid engineering is not responsible for this waxwork figure. The polished perfection of the marriage of head and candle depends on the lively interplay of textures and layering techniques to create this unusual portrait of a man melting under a candle flame. (Image: Michael Kerbow. Printbox)

Fig. 19 – 2. *Model photographed from front.*

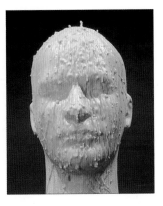

Fig. 19 – 3. *Mannequin head with melted wax photographed from the same position as the head.*

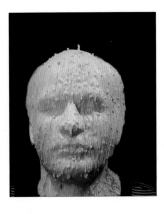

Fig. 19 – 4. *Both head shots are aligned.*

Fig. 19 – 5. *Color corrections were executed through stencils of the wax to create a solarized blown–out color shift to the flesh tones, adding to the illusion of wax.*

Fig. 19 – 6. *Stencil of model.*

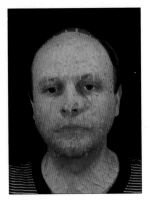

Fig. 19 – 7. *Overlay of wax on model.*

Fig. 19 – 8. *Photograph of rim of candle.*

INNERSCAPES

In these images, abstract forms, layering effects, and strategic lighting emerge to accent rhythm and movement. The complexity in the image comes from the play of colors, texturing, and atmospheric effects. (Image: Hye-Kyung Kim)

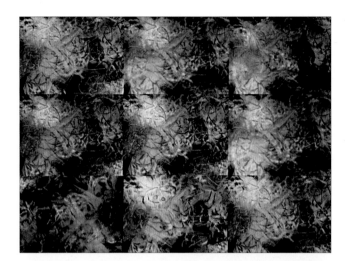

Fig. 20 a – 1. *Low resolution test of texture maps.*

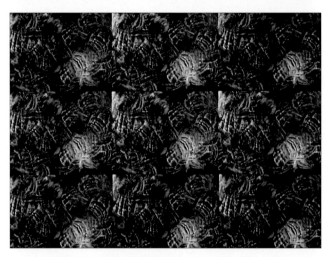

Fig. 20 b – 1. *Material definitions, texturing, color, lighting, and natural properties interact with various surfaces.*

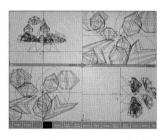

Fig. 20 c – 1. *Wireframe models of abstract forms.*

Fig. 20 c – 2. *Studies for surface quality and luminosity.*

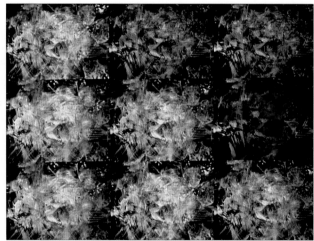

Fig. 20 d – 1. *Texture map studies affected by size, repetition, scale, and map rotation.*

TOM'S GREENHOUSE WINDOW

Using Polaroid instant film as a starting point, an impressionistic image of flowers is transformed by subtle and controlled effects in the paint program. The final piece resembles the dense impasto of an Impressionist master. (Image: David Scott Liebowitz: Detroit Digital Studios, Graphic Systems, and For-A)

Fig. 21 – 2. *Instant film is scanned into the computer using a drum scanner. The image is then repainted using a paint program.*

Fig. 21 – 1. *Original instant Polaroid film, exposed using a medium format camera*

Fig. 21 – 3. *The tumbler of flowers is then isolated from the overall composition and repainted again in the computer.*

Fig. 21 – 4. *An embossing technique is used to strengthen the idea of paint on canvas.*

Fig. 22 – 1. *Portrait of boy.*

Fig. 22 – 2. *Gallo-Roman funerary stele, second century A.D., Bourges, France.*

BOY IN A CHAIR

The elements that make up this portrait of a boy in a chair were all photographed on the same day. The light remains a constant throughout, whether it reflects from the surface of a pool or from the surface of the skin. This timeless image of childhood is reminiscent of the portraits by the French painter Balthus. The initial sketch was created with low-resolution files to speed up the creative process. The spontaneity of the original sketch was recreated using high-resolution files for the final output. (Image: Mary Lowenbach)

Fig. 22 – 3. *Swimming pool.*

Fig. 22 – 4. *Preliminary sketch with low-resolution files.*

Fig. 22 – 5. *Stencil of boy.*

Fig. 22 – 6. *The swimming pool image is placed on top of the stele.*

Fig. 22 – 7. *The boy is placed on top of the pool and the stele.*

Fig. 22 – 8. *The images are combined using high-resolution files and reversion and cloning.*

Fig. 22 – 9. *Polaroid transfer of sketch on rag paper.*

Fig. 22 – 10. *Polaroid transfer of sketch on rag paper.*

Fig. 22 – 11. *Color Laser print*

Fig. 22 – 12. *Polaroid print using adjusted filtration.*

FUNERARY STELE

In this image the work of a second-century sculptor is transformed with twentieth-century technology. The completed image appears as a fragment of a funerary stele. The original second century A.D. Gallo-Roman relief of a man's head is transformed into a skull using a morphing process. A knowledge of human anatomy and proportion is revealed through this process as the features of skull and head fuse seamlessly, bridging the centuries. (Image: Mary Lowenbach)

Fig. 23 – 1. *Gallo-Roman funerary stele, second century A.D., Bourges, France.*

Fig. 23 – 2. *Multiple niches created from stele.*

Fig. 23 – 3. *Gallo-Roman funerary stele of man from Bourges, France.*

Fig. 23 – 4. *Studio photograph of skull.*

Fig. 23 – 5. *The skull is masked and sized.*

Fig. 23 – 6. *Stone slab is cloned from the stele.*

Fig. 23 – 7. *Skull is placed on relief.*

Fig. 23 - 8. *72% skull—28% relief.*

Fig. 23 – 9. *63% skull—37% relief.*

Fig. 23 – 10. *54% skull—46% relief.*

Fig. 23 – 11. *45% skull—55% relief.*

Fig. 23 – 12. *36% skull—64% relief.*

Fig. 23 – 13. *27% skull—73% relief.*

Fig. 23 – 14. *18% skull—82% relief.*

 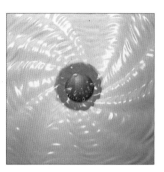 

Fig. 24 – 1. *Photograph of model, with filter effect to deform face.*

Fig. 24 – 2. *An image of a whirlpool in a sink is used as a reference to displace the image.*

Fig. 24 – 3. *The displace filter is applied to the first image. The effect of the filter is to displace each pixel in image 1 according to the brightness of each pixel in image 2.*

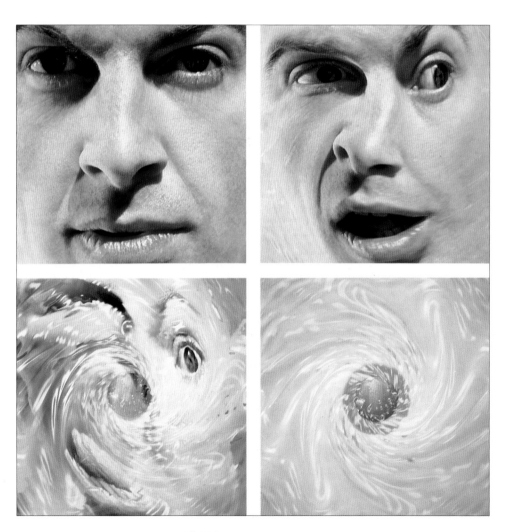

VORTEX

A powerful combination of 2D and 3D imagery is used in this creation of a face trapped in a vortex of flowing water. (Image: Sylvian Moreau)

Fig. 24 – 4. *A stencil is created.*

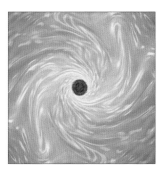

Fig. 24 – 5. *An image of a whirlpool is created.*

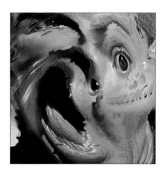

Fig. 24 – 6. *Image 5 is pasted onto image 3 through the stencil prepared in image 4.*

Fig. 24 – 7. *This stencil is created by converting a color image to black and white and adjusting the brightness and contrast.*

Fig. 24 – 8. *Image 5 is pasted on image 3 through the new mask. The plug in the sink is copied and pasted to create the final image.*

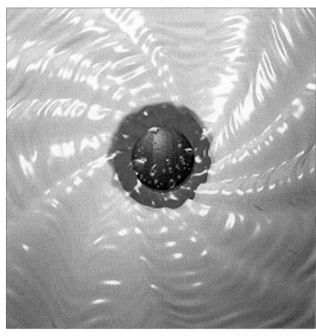

Fig. 24 – 9. *An image of a whirlpool in a sink is created in a 3D environment.*

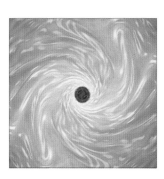

Fig. 24 – 10. *A twirl filter is applied to image 9.*

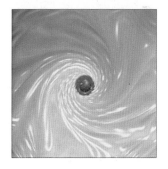

Fig. 24 – 11. *Image 10 is rotated by 180 degrees and pasted down on itself.*

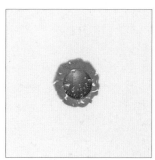

Fig. 24 – 12. *The plug in image 9 is pasted onto image 11.*

Fig. 25 – 1. *This photograph of the Flatiron Building was chosen because of its sharpness and the spontaneous movement of flags and random street activity. The lower right hand corner was toned down because of distracting highlights.*

Fig. 25 – 2. *A second shot of the Flatiron Building, taken from the same perspective, had darker, less distracting information in the same area, so it was cut and pasted into position. A third shot of yellow cabs was placed over other distractions, also adding more color.*

Fig. 25 – 3. *A photograph of a dramatic sky is used to create a mood. The original sky was cut out and replaced with this new sky. The information was inverted and color enhanced to make it look more threatening.*

Fig. 25 – 4. *A photograph of fireworks are used for the fork of lighting. An explosion at the center of a firework was isolated and placed at the designated breaking point in the final composition.*

BREAKING TRADITION

The "decisive moment" championed by Henry Gartier Bresson is here recreated using the computer. No photographer was on hand to capture the lightning striking the Flatiron Building in Manhattan. This decisive moment has been carefully constructed by selecting a variety of different photographs. The top section of the building was selectively isolated and repositioned to give the appearance of falling. Various pieces of debris were cloned from the main building in "rock-like" shapes and pasted into the sky to give the appearance of shrapnel. Recognizable signs and objects were obscured because they would have dated the image. (Image: Dennis Novak. Duggal)

Fig. 26 – 1. *The Twin Towers were electronically masked from their background and then selectively warped using distortion tools. They were then placed into position with additional overlapping to reinforce the illusion of space.*

Fig. 26 – 2. *The tornado was created by selectively isolating a pattern of clouds, distorting the information downward in a long, narrow channel toward a point, and then, after modifying colors, placing the information into the composition.*

Fig. 26 – 3. *The water in the final image combine the rolling waves of this photograph with the "white caps" of Fig. 27–4.*

Fig. 26 – 4. *More waves and New York Harbor are combined with the previous image to create a rough sea for the final composition.*

TWIN TOWERS

The World Trade Center in Manhattan is used as a background for an unlikely weather forecast. A tornado twists the twin towers into a knot. Final touches, including dust, debris, and fractured buildings, were added using cloning tools. (Image: Dennis Novak. Duggal)

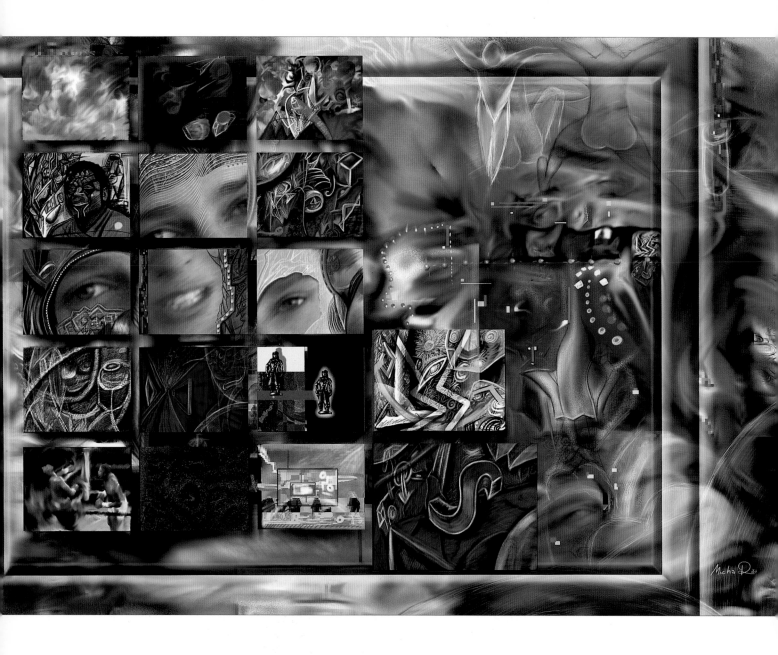

FRAMES OF MIND

*There is an unusual vocabulary of light in computer images; ordinary sunlight is
uncommon, and neon light and the light that comes in brilliantly artificial colors
are typical. Also common are color schemes that compliment each other but no
longer refer to a natural universe. In this image, fragments are digitally grafted
into a rough-cut mosaic representing different states of mind.
(Image: Micha Riss. M2)*

Fig. 27 – 2. *Floating form using a drop shadow.*

Fig. 27 – 1. *Black and white sketch.*

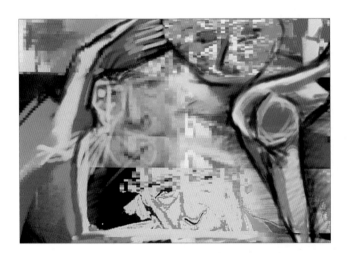

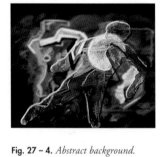

Fig. 27 – 4. *Abstract background.*

Fig. 27 – 3. *Portrait fragmented.*

Fig. 27 – 5. *Stylized graffiti.*

Fig. 28 – 1. *The Amolfini marriage by Jan Van Eyck.*

DIGITAL FAUX

The Arnolfini marriage by Jan Van Eyck is the first oil painting in history. The technique of underpainting with countless glazes of color created a rich and luminous realism that had never been seen before the sixteenth century. Many changes have been made to this famous icon. Other unlikely objects, including wristwatches for the bride and groom, were added, but in such a way as to retain the integrity of the original image. (Image: Patty Wongpakdee)

Fig. 28 – 2. *A new hat for the groom, which was colorized to match the tone of the original hat. Airbrushing was also used to make the hat more three dimensional, and finally it was scaled to replace the original hat in the picture.*

Fig. 28 – 3. *A bakelite radio for the shelf near the window, colorized to match the wood tones in the painting.*

Fig. 28 – 4. *A modern day kiwi fruit.*

Fig. 28 – 5. *Red shoes to replace the clogs in the original painting. Originally too bright, they were tinted to avoid a clash with the color.*

Fig. 28 – 6. *One of Albrecht Durer's drawings of a hare replaced the small dog in the foreground. The background was extended first to cover the dog.*

Fig. 28 – 7. *Electric light bulbs replace the candles in the chandelier. They were later blurred to diminish their hard contour.*

METAMORPHOSIS

Certain styles and techniques can be used to refer to photography's past. In the late 1840s and 1850s, photographers erected their tripods beside artists' easels in attractive landscape locations. When the first calotype and colloidion prints were produced, their technical qualities were reminiscent of this sepia landscape. In the completed image the potato was scaled and placed in the background, followed by the fork and then the figure. This required seamless retouching with the electronic airbrush, and then the whole image was washed with a sepia tone.
(Image: Patty Wongpakdee)

Fig. 29 – 1. *A photograph of trees was the initial inspiration for the atmosphere in this surreal environment.*

Fig. 29 – 3. *Photograph of fork in potato.*

Fig. 29 – 2. *"In the Woods," a painting by Asher B. Durand of the Hudson River School, was stretched and tinted for the background.*

Fig. 29 – 4. *Photograph of fork alone. Ultimately the fork was cut and pasted into a different location in the potato.*

Fig. 29 – 5. *The model is posed for alignment with the handle of the fork.*

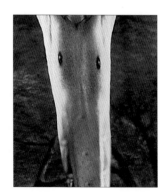

Fig. 29 – 6. *The torso of figure and the handle of the fork blended together.*

VENICE

This view of Venice has a magical air. It combines an evocative panoramic view with an unusual vantage point. The artist Canaletto captured eighteenth-century Venetian life in all its detail. He was able to arrive at these views, inaccessible to the human eye, by using a special device, the 'optical chamber,' which made it possible for an artist to obtain a faithful image of reality. Today's optical chamber, the graphics computer, allows the artist to render a tranquil view based on a photograph. (Image: Mieko Yoshida)

Fig. 30 – 1. *A black and white photograph of Venice.*

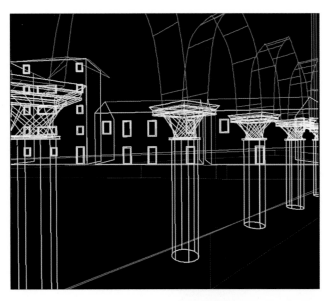

Fig. 30 – 2. *A wireframe model is constructed from the photograph to locate the viewpoint and composition.*

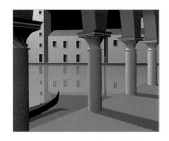

Fig. 30 – 3. *One ambient light and one spotlight are used to create the lighting in the scene.*

Fig. 30 – 4. *Bump mapping is used for the ripples in the canal and cubic environmental color mapping is used for subtle reflections.*

Fig. 30 – 5. *Ray tracing is used to create a strong shadow and reflections. No bump mapping or environmental mapping is used for the water.*

Fig. 30 – 6. *This image is a composite of earlier ones. Details in the house are eliminated to simplify the overall effect in the image. Only subtle color mapping is used for the houses. An emphasis on cool hues is replaced by warm ones in the final image.*

STAIRWAY

A strong sense of mystery is created through a subtle use of dramatic lighting in this series of studies featuring an industrial structure and water. The spectator casts a shadow on the stairway, adding to the nightmarish quality of the scene. Each study employs a filter effect or cloner brush. (Image: Mieko Yoshida)

Fig. 31 – 1. *The stairway is modeled using polygonal and skin data. The clouds are a primitive sphere, and the water is a primitive plane. The clouds employ transparency mapping. A cloud texture is mapped on several spheres. This is accomplished using a fractal algorithm, which is a random function with a specific frequency distribution. Fractals were applied for surface transparency mapping. The mapping went from completely opaque to completely transparent. The shadow is created using a spotlight.*

Fig. 31 – 2. *A cloner brush is used to create a stippled version of the image, evoking a pointillist style like that of Georges Seurat.*

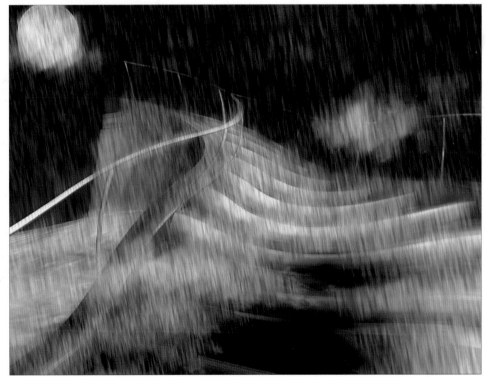

Fig. 31 – 3. *A texture is used to create a rugged painterly surface like impasto. The image looks like it has been sculpted from bold swirling brushstrokes. The raised areas catch the light, creating a lively and energetic surface.*

Fig. 31 – 4. *A texture is used to create a craquelure effect. (Craquelure is the cracks that appear in the surface of an oil painting as it ages.)*

Fig. 31 – 5. *A cloner brush is used to create a vibrant effect, scumbling together a dark and light crayon by cross hatching.*

Patricia Johnson and Jim Kilkelly

Still Video and Digital Camera Systems

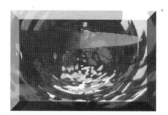

Still video and digital photography has begun to mature, with new offerings enhancing earlier ones. The underlying CCD chip technology has improved substantially, enabling the capture of images that are coming closer in quality to a continuous tone photograph. But the shift from silver halide to silicon, as it is now commonly called, is still a complex, confusing task.

Unfortunately, the dark side is that electronic photography never ends with the choice of camera alone. Conventional photography has evolved into a predictable "system" or series of steps employing various camera bodies, lenses, film, formats, and controlled chemical processes. The photographer selects the camera and the type of film. Once the film is exposed, there are some decisions that can be made in the processing, but the end of the imaging chain is at least close at hand. Digital photography calls into play a panorama of other technologies, in which the cameras are just the beginning link in the digital imaging chain.

Today the user must build a knowledge of video technology, computer hardware, computer software, image processing, file management, storage capabilities, color in the digital world, color calibration issues, output devices, electronic prepress, and a vocabulary with which to communicate with service bureaus. This knowledge base must be accompanied by an understanding of the performance of traditional cameras compared to digital cameras, including lens capabilities, reciprocity failure characteristics, and translations between the image performance of digital cameras as compared to conventional film performance. Finally this body of knowledge can be applied to individual photographic needs. Within the constraints of individual budgets and studio facilities, the appropriate camera (input device) can be selected for the job.

If this does not sound familiar, it is because it usually doesn't happen this way. More often than not, the opposite approach is taken. A camera is leased or purchased and the other issues unfold when stumbling blocks are reached or crises are overcome. What users are finding is that lack of information about any single variable in the digital photography process multiplies as the project proceeds.

What is needed is a method for sorting out each element of the electronic imaging process and relating it to the others. The following step-by-step approach offers such a method.

APPLICATIONS

The first questions to ask are what type of photography do you do, and what are the parameters of the job or jobs you will be shooting? The categories of photography are not easy to separate and often overlap. The equipment requirements vary with function and specific personal styles.

Product photography for sales brochures demand crisp high-quality images, while run-of-press inserts may have lesser demands. Illustration photography for advertising, food, or editorial work has a range of requirements that include a large number of lens and large-format cameras. These shots would be done in a studio using tripods and lights. Photojournalists generally need portability, ruggedness, and ease of use. At times, however, speed of processing or fast access to images can be critical. Fine art photographers have few time constraints and encounter no rigid style parameters. In-house photography, which includes a wide range of uses, demands equipment that is adaptable to many different applications.

In short, form follows function, and defining the job you want to do immediately narrows choices and simplifies the process of selection.

The best way to get a feel for specific cameras is to test them. Most of these systems can be leased for reasonable rates and tested for suitability.

BUDGET

It is often difficult to set a budget for equipment that is unfamiliar. However, determining financial parameters can assist greatly in the selection process. Understanding the technology aids in understanding the financial issues involved in electronic photography. This is a good illustration of how the parts of the selection process are dependant on one another.

There are some rules of thumb that can help determine budget issues. Remember, digital photography is dependent on computer capabilities. A traditional photographer creates a positive or negative image on film. The electronic photographer creates a file. It can be a real drawback to choose the highest resolution camera because the size of the image files created in high-end cameras can strain the computer resources that will support it.

Processing the computer file is an expense. This stage of the imaging chain will require an investment either in a desk top computing system or in leased time on a commercial system such as the Diamond Imaging System, Kodak Premier, or Scitex.

Storage of large image files is a primary concern. The cost of high volume storage devices is high and must be built into the budget.

Prepress costs are also a consideration. Sony is claiming that their SEPS 1000 Studio System is more cost effective by a ratio of 20 to 1 compared with traditional methods. According to their findings, conventional prepress processes that took 2.5 hours can be done in the electronic environment in 7.5 minutes.

The main thing to remember is that there is more to consider than the cost of the camera alone. The most effective way to approach the financial questions is to gain an understanding of the technology.

THE DIGITAL IMAGING CHAIN

- -

There are three basic types of cameras on the market now—still video, digital instant type, and digital scanning type. Images from these cameras vary as to resolution of the image (the number of pixels—picture elements—of information which give detail), color quality, and image capture time which ranges from instantaneous to twelve minutes. One of the most interesting things about digital photography, though, is that these cameras sometimes function so differently from conventional cameras that there is no established vocabulary with which to describe them. This is another reason to become familiar enough with the camera technology and the components of the digital imaging chain to be able to ask the appropriate questions. The following overview will outline some of these concepts. While this survey is not intended to give detailed technical information, it will provide the basis for a comprehensive list of questions users should ask and the reasons for asking them.

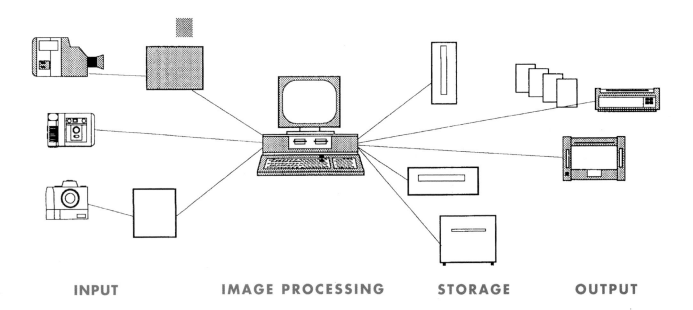

INPUT　　　　**IMAGE PROCESSING**　　　　**STORAGE**　　　　**OUTPUT**

CCDs

Very simply, light entering the camera lens strikes "photoreceptors" on a CCD (charge-coupled device). A CCD is a silicon chip that is etched with special circuitry, coated with photoconductive material, and housed in a casing.

There are several types of CCDs, but they all function by measuring the analog qualities of light (photons) and converting this information into a measurement of voltage (electrons).

In a color still video or digital camera the number of CCDs, the method used to filter the light, the time it will take to capture the image, the amount of data that is captured, and the manner in which it is converted to a digital file determines the quality of the image which will result. Ultimately the result defines the usefulness of the camera.

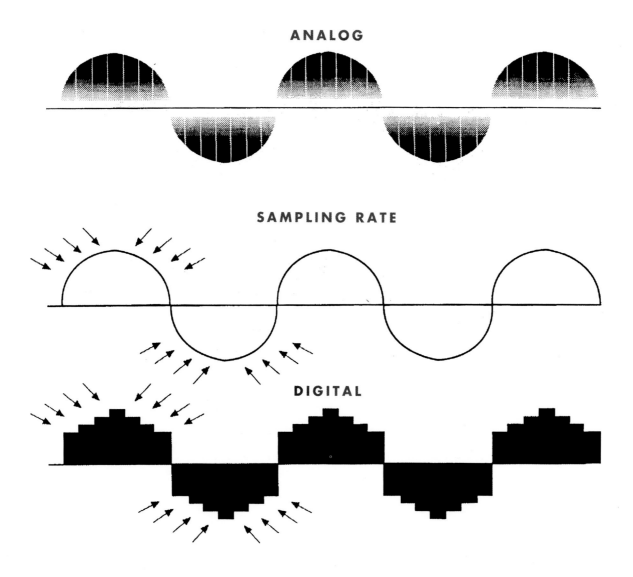

ANALOG

SAMPLING RATE

DIGITAL

Analog to Digital

Light (*analog* or *photons*) is converted into magnetic impulses, or measurements of voltage (*analog* or *electrons*) called "packets." These packets are transferred by various means into the circuitry of the camera systems, after which they are converted to image files in the computer (*digital*).

IMAGE CAPTURE

Light entering the camera lens forms a pattern on sensors in an "array" (an *ordered arrangement, table, or pattern of items or numbers*) of pixels or picture elements; a microscopic grid that captures information about the amount and quality of light that strikes each of its elements. The easiest way to visualize a CCD array is to imagine a mosaic made up of thousands of tiny adjacent vertical and horizontal rows of rectilinear points.

There is much to learn about the complexity of CCDs. Basically there are three types of CCDs, each with different attributes and suited for different types of cameras.

Interline transfer CCDs *scan* the array and interleave the capture and storage functions, a process that yields image information on only about one-third of the total pixel area. These provide better color than do other types of CCDs.

Frame-transfer CCDs capture and store information in two separate steps. These provide high accuracy.

Matrix CCDs, in which all pixels are read sequentially, provide greater speed.

One important rule of thumb to remember is that the aspect ratio of the chip does not equate to the aspect ratio of the film format, so the viewfinder is inaccurate and therefore masked. This means, for example, that in a digital 35mm camera that accepts multiple lenses, a 50 mm focal length lens considered normal in film mode becomes in effect a 100 mm focal length telephoto lens in the digital world.

COLOR

In color CCDs the full spectrum of light entering the camera lens must be separated into the three additive colors (red, blue, and green) to be used in the digital environment. In the three CCD cameras, the beam of full spectrum of light is split into three and filtered, and each color is read on a separate chip. The single CCD camera utilizes a color filter array that is placed over the face of the chip to separate light into its red, green, and blue components.

The method of filtering color has a significant effect on the quality of the image. Single-chip cameras can be made smaller and more portable, but this method of calculating color can contribute to certain anomalies in the resulting image. However, the application for such cameras, specifically photojournalism, is not affected by these anomalies and is greatly benefited by the portability and speed of the cameras.

A major issue for concern is how color changes from input to processing to output. There are currently several color calibration devices and software packages that can offer some measure of control over this aspect of the imaging chain, but the best solution is to close the loop—in other words, to install the entire chain and calibrate each device to each other and to the whole. By controlling the entire loop themselves, users can gain the most predictable and repeatable results. If a service bureau is used as part of the loop, find a good one, establish a method of communication, and stick with them for consistency.

A three-chip camera is larger and therefore limited as to use, but it can capture high-quality color information. This camera is ideally suited for product shots and other studio applications.

Judging image quality has much to do with the viewing distance, type of reproduction, and other applications issues. Understanding the workings of the camera can help in predicting some of these variables.

FILE MANAGEMENT AND STORAGE

Digital photographs can create huge computer files. To work with them the computer requires two to three times as much memory as the file itself because the mathematical calculations of image processing are complex and memory intensive. Working with these images can be a slow process if there is no acceleration built into the computer doing the processing. Purchase or lease of a fully loaded desk top imaging system is costly. The actual needs of the user should determine if this investment is the right one.

There are now CCD chips that are able to capture up to 6,000,000 pixels of information. The most powerful digital cameras now on the market capture approximately 1,360,000 pixels. But never will a resulting digital image retain all this information. There is always some information lost in converting the captured image into digital form so the pixel capacity of the array does not translate in a one-to-one ratio with the digital file in the computer.

One of the most difficult aspects of defining a digital photograph by the number of pixels in the image is that some manufacturers describe the image file in terms of X and Y coordinates, others in pixels per inch, and still others in file sizes and scan lines. In some ways file size is actually the most pertinent measurement because it will lead to decisions about the internal and external storage needs within the imaging chain.

STILL VIDEO

Still video systems store images in analog form on two-inch floppy disks equivalent to the video recording on a camcorder. This analog information is then converted to digital (binary) form through an internal or external player. Information can be lost in this two-step process.

Some still video cameras acquire the image in either the field or the frame mode. These terms relate to video technology. In video the signal is scanned onto the image area in two passes—even lines in one pass and odd lines in the other. In frame mode all video lines are filled with acquired image information in two passes. The field mode acquires data in every other line only. The remaining lines are filled in by mathematical calculation or interpolations from the acquired information. This interpolated information then fills in the empty lines. Frame mode results in larger files with better image quality. Field mode allows for twice as many images of lower image quality.

Another carryover from video is that some still video cameras describe light in lux, which is a video term.

PHOTO CD

- -

The technology is now available to transfer images taken with a conventional camera onto an optical compact disk. Once the images are stored, the digital picture file can be read by a computer using a suitable CD-ROM drive. Once the image is brought onto the desktop of the computer it can be manipulated with any of the available image-editing programs. An excellent medium for archiving images, photo CD turns scanning photographs for digital photo illustration into several easy steps.

J . N e v i n   S h a f f e r ,   J r .

No One Owns
The Sunset

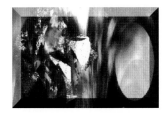

When Duchamp questioned the viability of valuing high art on the basis of unique authorship, he could not have imagined a more perfect producer of "readymades" than a database.

State-of-the-art CEPS have powerful image-processing capabilities and bring with them a potential Pandora's box of legal problems. Responsible users of this state-of-the-art image processing equipment must never lose sight of the legal rights of others in the excitement of using this equipment. Although processes for creating, enhancing, and modifying images have changed, a large body of law exists that is pertinent to the creation of original artwork regardless of the technology that is prevalent.

BASIC RULES OF THE GAME

It is possible that an operator can get the sense that even ownership is untenable:

that someone's creation—perhaps a shape or a file—can be used by someone else without the creator ever missing it. As if by magic, the raw material will never be depleted by use!

The United States Constitution calls for protection of "writings of authors." The copyright laws of the United States seek to promote literary and artistic creativity by protecting certain works for a limited time. The owner of a copyrighted work is given *exclusive* rights to reproduce the work, to distribute the reproductions, to display and perform it publicly, t*o prepare derivative works based on it*, and to authorize others to do any of these things. Before 1978, copyright protection lasted for twenty-eight years and could be renewed for another twenty-eight years. Any work published or disclosed publicly without the three elements of a copyright notice (the copyright symbol or the word "copyright," the year of first publication, and the copyright owner's name) might, under certain circumstances, enter the "public domain"; that is become public property.

Works published after 1978 are protected for the life of the author plus fifty years. If the copyright owner is an unamed author or an employer, the copyright will last for one hundred years from its creation or seventy-five years from publication, whichever is earlier. The punitive requirement of making authors place the copyright notice on their works or lose their rights has been removed for works published after 1978. The law now provides protection to authors the instant their work is reduced to a tangible form, even though that work does not carry the copyright notice. As a result, if the author can prove he or she created the subject work, even though the copyright notice was not attached to it, he or she can force another individual to stop producing, reproducing, or selling infringing works. Operators, therefore, must be very careful when considering using works lacking a copyright notice without thoroughly researching its origin.

Post-1978 authors are still motivated to place the copyright notice on their works and obtain registration, because with such notice and registration their works are fully protected by law. That is, once they are registered authors may not only stop an individual from producing infringing works, but they may receive statutory damages, court costs, and attorney's fees as well. As a practical matter, then, knowledgeable authors will attach the copyright notice to their works and register them as a matter of course.

INNOCENCE IS NO EXCUSE

Under the copyright law, a person who creates an infringing work from an image he or she did not realize was protected is still guilty of infringement. All the copyright owner must show is that he or she is the owner of the copyright in issue, that the protected work was infringed upon by the image processor, and that the author has been damaged as a result. As a result, anyone processing images needs to know copyright laws so that they carefully analyze the image they are working with and determine whether or not it has a copyright notice.

THE COPYING OF COPYRIGHTED WORK
IS AN INFRINGEMENT

A work is presumed by the courts to have been infringed upon—copied—if the author can prove that the infringer, for example the person operating the CEPS, had access to the copyrighted work and that there is a "substantial similarity" between the two.

Some courts define access as actual viewing of a work by the defendant operator. The majority view, however, is that the author need only prove the operator had a "reasonable opportunity" to see the protected image. The requirement of showing access is an attempt by the courts to remove the possibility of coincidence concerning the creation of identical works, since identical works, *if independently created*, can both be protected under the copyright laws. If, however, the author can show that the operator had access or that there are so many similarities between the two works that independent creation is precluded and a presumption of access may be inferred, the defense of independent creation will be rejected.

Finally, the *author must show substantial similarity between his or her protected work and your processed image in order to prevail.* A strict definition of "substantial similarity" is not possible since each alleged infringement is taken on a case-by-case basis. The totality of the circumstances are evaluated to determine whether the rights of the author under the copyright laws have been infringed. If the only difference is that the operator removed the copyright notice from the infringed work, then infringement has obviously occurred. If no similarities exist between the processed image and the protected work, then no infringement exists. Between these two extremes, however, a case-by-case subjective analysis will be made. Knowledge of these basic rules should allow an operator to recognize opportunities to be had and pitfalls to be avoided.

WHAT IF THE WORK TO BE PROCESSED IS IN THE PUBLIC DOMAIN?

If the operator knows the particular image he or she is working on is in the public domain and free of protection by copyrights, then he or she may process the image without fear of infringement. Indeed, once the processing is complete, the user should consider registering the copyright in the original work he or she has created. The process for registration is straightforward, the work may be registered in an unpublished form, and the filing fee is $20.00. Once the work is published, it may be registered in published form, using the same application format, for an additional $20.00. Forms are available from and applications should be made to the Register of Copyrights, Library of Congress, Washington D.C. 20599. Operators should insert the copyright notice on all original works and copies they create and make a habit of registering their copyrights in their original works.

WHAT IF THE IMAGE TO BE PROCESSED IS PROTECTED?

The safest way to proceed with a protected work, of course, is to obtain permission from the copyright owner. Even with permission, however, operators are wise to pass processed images by the copyright owner for secondary approval of the resultant work. Operators should also keep in mind that what is protected by the author's copyright is the author's expression of an idea and *not the idea itself.* If the idea and the expression are congruent, then little or no protection exists and perhaps even an almost exact copying of the "protected work" would not be an infringement. On the other hand, if the idea and the expression of the idea are not identical, but are subject to a wide variety of expressions, then more care should be taken in processing that particular image.

HOW MUCH CHANGE AVOIDS INFRINGEMENT?

This is the million dollar question. It should be clear by now that the gist of copyright infringement is the unauthorized utilization of that part of the work that is protected. That is to say, once again, the expression by a particular author of a specific idea is what is protected. The general theme of the idea is not protected by any one copyright. Every operator is free to create his or her own image, for example, of a sunrise behind the Golden Gate Bridge. Still, no operator is allowed to copy another author's protected expression of the same idea. Courts will look at the processed image and attempt to determine whether it represents a "substantial similarity" between the processed image and the protected work. Further, the courts will consider the total circumstances in an effort to determine on a case-by-case basis whether substantial similarity exists between the protected work and the allegedly infringing work. Because scanning an image into the system may, by itself, technically constitute illegal copying, without regard to the amount of manipulation of the image, it is best to tread this ground very carefully.

SAFE PROCESSING GUIDELINES

Know your source and protect your own works. An initial determination that the basic image to be processed is either free from copyright or in the public domain makes issues of copyright infringement moot. Further, image processors should obtain protection for any original work they produce and establish routine procedures for doing so.

If it's protected, get permission. Once you have permission from the owner of a copyrighted work, image processing may proceed. Operators should make clear to the author what the purpose and expected result will be, and, as a matter of caution, provide an opportunity for the original author to inspect the processed work before publication, even after getting permission.

Without written permission, proceed very cautiously. An analysis of the protected work should be made to determine the extent of the protection afforded that particular work. Operators must remember that protection extends to expressions of ideas only and not to the idea itself. The fundamental test for infringement is substantial similarity between the two works, and the court will consider the totality of the idea presented in an effort to make this determination. The capabilities of state-of-the-art image processing are truly remarkable and surely will increase. While an operator's ability to reproduce, modify, and amend images increases, however, the prohibition against unauthorized reproduction of protected images remains constant. A prudent operator will understand the rights afforded under copyright law so that he or she may protect his or her own original work while avoiding trespassing on protected rights of others.

SUMMARY

The protection afforded under copyright law is narrow in the sense that a protected work is only protected to the extent it is an original expression of an idea. The idea itself is not protected. Because the protection is narrow, a person found guilty of copyright infringement is dealt with harshly and can expect to pay court costs, damages, and attorney's fees. Unfortunately, there is no black and white rule that that can be used to measure whether there is "substantial similarity" between the copyrighted work and the processed image. This is a matter decided by judge or jury. At a minimum, though, an operator should be convinced that no substantial similarity exists, at least in his or her own mind, between the processed image and the source image. Certainly, the safest procedure is to start with works in the public domain or works originally created by the operator on the computer.

Obviously this article is no substitute for competent legal advice concerning the unique circumstances individual operators will face. Since there are other overlapping rights given individuals and businesses, including the rights of publicity, trade dress, and trademark, such legal advice is recommended for any operator who intends to manipulate images, particularly if those images are going to be published or broadcast.

Endnotes

1. Image digitization and manipulation go by a variety of names, including computer, digital, or electronic imaging or retouching; computer enhancement; and electronic color imaging (ECI). Associated processes are sometimes referred to as the electronic darkroom. This laser-based technology may employ scanners to convert already existing still images into digital information, or information may be garnered in digital form from electronic cameras or camera elements.

2. In 1966, *Life* magazine opened its 30th anniversary issue, a special double issue entitled "Photography," with a rumination on photographic truth, including this quoted remark by James Agee: ". . . it is doubtful whether most people realize how extraordinarily slippery a liar the camera is. The camera is just a machine, which records with impressive and, as a rule, very cruel faithfulness precisely what is in the eye, mind, spirit, and skill of its operators to make it record." *Life* comments, recuperatively: ". . . it is entirely possible for a skilled photographer to twist the truth to his liking. . . . To use this power well requires a strong conscience, and the best photographers suffer its burden. . . . [But] who would say that a photograph should just mirror life. . . . And which man among us holds the one, true mirror?" *Life,* Vol. 61, No. 26 (Dec. 23,1966), p. 7.

3. Although an essay of mine on the institutionalization of documentary photography ("In, Around, and Afterthoughts: On Documentary Photography," in *Martha Rosler: 3 Works* [Halifax: Press of the Nova Scotia College of Art and Design, 1981]) has been taken to support the idea that "documentary is dead," I believe, on the contrary, that documentary is alive—if those who do it exercise responsibility in their decisions relating to the production, dissemination, and marketing of their images. Not that voluntarism is the answer, but I don't think we are will-less creatures, either.

4. Among other images in Charles Darwin, *The Expression of Emotion in Man and Animals.* (See the 1965

reprint by the University of Chicago Press. No date is offered for the original, but other sources suggest 1872.)

5. See Jorge Lewinski, *The Camera al War* (New York: Simon and Schuster, 1978), pp. 83–92; and Phillip Knightley, *The First Casualty* (New York: Harcourt, 1975), pp. 209–12.

6. See Karal Ann Marling and John Wetenhall, *Monuments, Memories and the American Hero* (Cambridge: Harvard University Press, 1991), and its review by Richard Severo, "Birth of a National Icon, but an Illegitimate One" *(New York Times,* October 1, 1991).

7. The resulting image, made after the Battle of Gettysburg, is generally known as *Dead Confedera-e Soldier at Sharpshooter's Position in Devil's Den, 1863,* but it is also sometimes identified as *Home of Rebel Sharpshooter.* For a brief discussion, see Howard Bossen, "Zone V: Photojoumalism, Ethics, and the Electronic Age," *Studies in Visual Communication,* Vol 7, No. 3 (Summer, 1985), p. *22 ff.*

8. See Robert E. Sobieszek, *The Architectural Photography of Hedrich-Blessing* (New York: Henry Holt, 1984).

9. See Eric Barnouw's *Magician and the Cinema* (New York: Oxford, 1981) for an account of the relationship between magic and the cinema.

10. Niépce, the other inventor, was interested in reproducing images of already existing art prints, to facilitate their sale and improve profitability.

11. Quoted in the *New York Times* for August 15, 1991, in a brief discussion of the exhibition "Site Work, Architecture in Photography Since Early Modemism," at the Photographers' Gallery in London, and in Janet Abrams' catalogue essay for that show.

12. "Michael Radencich," *Studio Light,* No. 1 (1988), pp. 2–10. See next note.

13. It isn't clear why someone wouldn't just as soon do most of the work on a computer. Perhaps the far greater

resolution of film still tells, though the computer is getting better and better. But a fascination with the microcosm, with real table-top models and miniatures, has pervaded photography, film, and video—particularly, though not only, that made by men.

Kodak, of course, to avoid extinction, is now aggressively pursuing the image-processing market; it offers a case-in-point of corporate retoolingt—if you can't beat 'em, join 'em. In fact, it now refers to its industry not as "photography" but as "imaging," and it calls digital manipulation "image enhancement." It has married one of its systems, Premier, to the graphics-friendly Macintosh computer, and it uses its various professionally oriented publications to promote electronic imaging, including "virtual reality" (see further on in the text). It has a number of products designed to keep film in the equation while allowing for digital operations between input and "hard copy" output. In 1991 it established the "Center for Creative Imaging" ("where art and technology meet") under the aegis of Raymond DeMoulin, general manager of Kodak's professional division. Sample remark from DeMoulin, in the summer 1992 course catalogue: "In the fifteenth century Gutenberg democratized—and universalized—publishing. Early in this century George Eastman enabled every man and woman to capture images photographically. Today, we face the millennium and a world of new media and technologies that are interactive and highly accessible. Kodak continues to embrace the challenge." Historical accuracy bows to inflated corporate claims. In the same catalogue, John Sculley, former CEO of Apple, Inc., writes: "Camden, Maine [where the center is located], feels a bit like Florence in the Renaissance."
14. "Even in the so-called photojournalist's magazine, in the much revered *National Geographic, I* have been witness to many, many contrived pictures. Of course, they say that those pictures reflect what actually happened, but wasn't happening at that moment. And so they had to fake it, right? Well, that's really beside the point. We have to question their integrity." Richard Steedman, stock-photo supplier, edited transcript of panel remarks at the Maine Photographic Workshops, "What's Selling in the Stock Photography Market," *PhotolDesign* (Jan./Feb., 1989), published by the Maine Photographic Workshops in support of its yearly photo conference and roundtable.

On the other hand, Rich Clarkson, director of photography at *National Geographic* and past president of the National Press Photographers Association, commented in another context: "Sometimes we pose pictures. I think it's very important that the reader understand what the situation is. . . . Sometimes in a caption we can explain that we organized these people to have this picture taken in a certain way. Or in the style of the photograph, it is so obviously posed that no reader is fooled into thinking that this was a real event." In "Discussion Group: Impromptu Panel Questions

Integrity of News Photography, Worries about Electronic Retouching," *News Photographer* (Jan., 1987), p. 41. These remarks don't really address Steedman's concerns and worries, however.

Instances of crude manipulation—a time-honored tradition in the tabloids—are easy to find in publications of the *Weekly World News* variety; we probably aren't *really* supposed to believe that the two warring stars in the photo (or, in another scenario, the two unexpectedly romancing stars) were actually photographed together—everything is *as if.* And sometimes their heads don't even fit their bodies. But the *reputable* press isn't supposed to indulge in these things, so eyebrows were raised when (for example) Raisa Gorbachev and Nancy Reagan (fulfilling either scenario outlined above) were pasted together in Time-Life's *Picture Week* for Nov. 25, 1985, or Tom Cruise and Dustin Hoffman in *Newsweek* in 1988. When an illustrator doing talk-show host Oprah Winfrey for the cover of *TV Guide* for August 25–Sep. 1, 1989, married Oprah's head to actress Ann-Margret's body, his faithfulness to the photograph from which he cribbed the body was so extreme that the man who had, six years earlier, designed Ann-Margret's gown recognized it and called her husband, who recognized Ann-Margret's ring on "Oprah's" finger. The *Guide's* editor assured everyone that the illustrator had been spoken to and that such a thing would never happen again—so recognizably, that is. My only glimpse of this cover before a report about it on National Public Radio's evening news program *All Things Considered* on August 30, 1989, was at a supermarket check-out counter, and I thought it was a photo.
15. For example, it is not clear even how definitive—or even how admissable—photographic evidence can be—without questions of digital manipulation (or indeed any kind of manipulation). Is it substantive and can it stand alone, or can it only be accepted as corroborative of the testimony of a human observer? A brief discussion of the fatal problem this posed for street-corner trafficsurveillance cameras in Canada is presented in "Plainclothes Cameras" (unsigned), in *Photo Communique,* Winter 1986/87.
16. Scitex, an Israeli-based company founded by engineer Efraim Arazi, saw the bulk of its early business in producing patterns for automated knitting and weaving machines; its attempt to enter—and dominate—the "printing-publishing-packaging" field did not begin until 1979 or 1980. Its major boost came from USA *Today's* heavy reliance on its system. "Prepress" production had been labor-intensive, time-consuming, and very expensive; Scitex put in the hands of a single operator (not necessarily one trained in earlier cut-paste-and-airbrush methods of image production) the ability to take an image from its "raw" state to its desired final form, and in very short order indeed. Although Scitex led the way, it was quickly followed by Dr-Ing Rudolph Hell, a subsidiary of the West German conglomerate

Siemens, which produces the Chromacom system, and by the Crosfield electronics subsidiary of the English De La Rue Group. (There are now other manufacturers as well.) Since the explosive development of this industry, many of these companies have been bought, sold, or merged. For example, the press manufacturer Linotype merged with Hell in 1991, and, according to *Fortune's* cover story "The New Look of Photography" (July 1, 1991), Du Pont and Fuji jointly bought Crosfield for $370 million in 1989.

Arazi's story is interesting. Having learned electronics in the Israeli military, Arazi went on to study at the Massachusetts Institute of Technology in the early 1960s and then worked on Boston's high-tech Route 128 for Itek, an image-technology company. Itek helped sponsor Scitex's start-up in Israel. One of the company's early projects, before entering the textile field, was the use of satellite technology during the Vietnam war to detect the Viet Cong on the basis of their "pajamas." (See the *New York Times* for Dec. 28, 1980, business section p. 7.) In 1992, Arazi was mentioned as president and CEO of a firm called Electronics for Imaging in San Bruno, California, and was quoted as saying "Photo CD [a Kodak imaging system based on compact disks] is God's gift to man" *(Business Publishing* [formerly *Personal Publishing*], April, 1992).

17. Personal communication.

18. I'll leave out the issue of envy here that, interestingly, operates in both directions. (The issue is who has what kind of power—if the professional photographer envies the creative autonomy and perhaps the fame and fortune of the art photographer, the artist, of course, envies the professional photographer's wide audience.)

The issue of copyright is not trivial with respect to electronic imaging, however—by and large, the client, not the photographer, holds the copyright on images produced for hire and can manipulate the Hell (or the Scitex, or the Mac) out of the image without obtaining the photographer's consent. More photojournalists than (other sorts of) commercial photographers are likely to retain the rights to their images. Some photographers are leading a movement toward having the photographer retain those rights. A similar issue of control has surfaced in relation to art, where the concept of the artistic integrity of a work is used to challenge a buyer's right to dispose of it as s/he sees fit. In 1992 Kodak, through its new Center for Creative (that is, digital) Imaging, published *Ethics, Copyright, and the Bottom Line,* based on a one-day symposium. It is predictable that a new standard of control over the image (that is, of property rights) will have to be developed in the courts, not only because of digital imaging but because of widespread cultural practices of incorporating previously produced material, such as "sampling" in rap music and hip hop. The standards established in the nineteenth century in relation to photographic production, for example, may give way to a twenty-first-century conception of property

and personhood. See Bernard Edelman, *Ownership of the Image.*

19. Anne M. Russell, "Digital Watch," *American Photographer,* Vol.16, No. 6 (June, 1986), p. 20. While it may be true that the industry has "so far demonstrated little love for technology," love isn't what motivates technological change. Stock-image libraries may not be fully converted to digitization, but the technology continues to make significant inroads, and National Digital appears to be doing quite well. According to the *Photo DistrictNews* (September, *1988),* NDCs "Photo Management Workstation" is in use at U.S. *News & World Report, Newsweek,* Houghton Mifflin, and several important stock agencies. At that time, NDC was also gearing up to use its scanning technology and a new portable work station at the Olympics, planning to produce digitized images from stationary or video sources in three to twenty seconds and transmit them over phone lines in fifteen to ninety seconds.

20. Including, say, *Time* magazine, which since mid-1991 has done its prepress on a Mac-Scitex combination, and every small publisher which has the Macintosh or IBM-compatible computer.

21. According to an interview with Jackie Greene, director of photography at *USA Today,* reported in Shiela *(sic)* Reaves's careful inside-the-industry article "'Digital Retouching," *News Photographer* (January, *1987), p. 27.(News Photographer is* published by the National Press Photographers Association, which accounts for the apparent care with which this issue, which contains a number of considerations of digitization, was researched and assembled.) Reaves's article, based on her studies and interviews, reports that *USA Today* tells all its 584 freelance photographers exactly how and what to use for each assignment, from the ASA to the fill flash. It also reports that *USA Today* helped with the research and development of portable Scitex transmitters, of which it now has exclusive use. These transmitters use either telephone wires (taking 3 1/2 minutes) or satellites (30 seconds) to transmit color photos to headquarters. All the newspaper personnel Reaves interviewed eschewed the use of their digitizing equipment for anything other than color correction and the enhancement of printability (whatever that means) *in news photos.* Interestingly, although the *Chicago Tribune* now uses digitizing procedures, Jack Com, its director of photography, is quoted as saying that before his tenure in the job, all photos were routinely retouched, but that no longer happens without approval.

22. Tom Hubbard, "AP Photo Chief, AEJMC Professors Discuss Ethics, Electronic Pictures at Convention," Higher Education column, News Photographer (January, 1987), p. 34. "AEJMC" stands for "Association for Education in Journalism and Mass Communication." Invoking Smith in this context is not without its perils: In American Photographer (July, 1989), John Loengard, former Life staffer, recalls his discovery after Smith's

death that the famous portrait of Albert Schweitzer as Great White Father in fact was something of a composite. Smith had introduced a couple of somewhat extraneous elements into the lower right-hand corner. Smith had kept this a carefully hidden secret, even making up a cover story about the negative. Loengard, calling his story "Necessary Cheating," writes "I understand and approve of what he did . . . even a photographer of his legendary sincerity felt driven to cheat a bit when he found his subject wasn't up to snuff." In contrast, U.S. Farm Security Administration photo head Roy Stryker emphatically disapproved of Dorothea Lange's removal of a minor element (a thumb) from that troublesome lower right-hand comer of her even more famous photograph, *Migrant Mother, Nipomo, California, 1936,* occasioning a bitter exchange of letters between Stryker and Lange. See Jack F. Hurley, *Porlrait of a Decade: Roy Stryker and the Development of Documentary Photography in the Thirties* (Baton Rouge: Louisiana State University Press, 1972; reprinted, New York: Da Capo, 1977). These examples can be variously interpreted, but Smith and Lange were intending to keep control of the images themselves, while Stryker, who apparently had no second thoughts about sending photographers into the field with shooting scripts (though not, of course, intending to have them pose photos) could not accept the photographer's quasi-aesthetic decision to manipulate an image after it was produced.

23. Roger Armbrust, "Computer Manipulation of the News," *Computer Pictures* (Jan/ Feb, 1985), pp. 6–114. The author spoke with representatives of the three "major television networks."

24. I feel compelled to mention, though, that the editor of this series, which began with *A Day in the Life of Australia,* is Rick Smolan, a photographer who conjured up the Australia project as a freelance package in 1980–81. Its cover showed some minor manipulation about equivalent to the other examples I've raised. Subsequently, according to a note in a 1992 Kodak publication, Smolan went on to train on its digital-imaging equipment and is now associated with the Kodak imaging center.

25. Though evidently not disinformation. As to readability, the initial photos, taken through the belly of a U-2 reconnaissance plane, required the deciphering abilities of highly trained photo interpreters. The photos finally exhibited were taken from very low-flying airplanes. The account in *Life* (Richard V. Stolley, "The Indispensable Camera," *Life,* Vol. 61, No. 26 [Dec. 23, 1966], pp. 98–100) offers no hint that military computer-assisted "enhancement" or interpretation systems were being developed, but the information presented in note 15 suggests otherwise.

26. This story was documented by Susan Meiselas.

27. Japanese or not, the list of corporations that have produced or expressed the desire to produce electronic still-imaging apparatuses—which actually includes Konica, Copal, Fuji, Hitachi, Nikon, Matsushita, and Mitsubishi, and the European companies Rollei Fototechnic and Arca Swiss, as well as Kodak and Polaroid—pits photographic firms against video and electronics manufacturers. Early versions of these apparatuses, such as Sony's Mavica, Canon's Xapshot, and Fuji's Fujix, while of use for small publications, haven't been successful in the consumer market because their prices are high, the image resolution is poor, and the outcome less interesting than video to the consumer. The various manufacturers are at work on higher resolution, more flexible devices—and among the major photographic manufacturers, Polaroid had better run to catch up. To that end, it has hired as director of research the former head of "innovative science and technology" for the government's so-called Star Wars program, the Strategic Defense Initiative. We must imagine the day when the stand-alone photography firm—like the stand-alone newspaper company or telephone company—that is not also involved in something electronic is obsolete. See John Holusha,"American Snapshot, the Next Generation," The *New York Times* (June 7,1992), business section, p.l: "Kodak and friends are betting that film is the key. Sony and Canon think otherwise" and "Photo cd is critical to the future of Kodak."

28. Digitization techniques are also used to enhance the readability of existing (usually still) images, most often by reducing blur, and one photo manufacturer is at work on a home-market application. Compare the Agfa slide printer described a bit further on in the same paragraph.(Agfa too is working on digitization applications and developments.)

A stumbling block in the mass marketing of imageprocessing programs has been the tremendous size of the computer files generated by images, but advances in image-compression programs and the tumbling cost of high-memory microprocessors (home computers) have greatly alleviated this problem. Such programs are now available for the IBM system as well as the Macintosh, and the cost is not much more than for a wordprocessing program. By 1991, estimates of graphics software sales lay between $160 million and $275 million (*New York Times,* May 17,1992). Because most such programs come with a library of images, called "clip art," copyright problems may ensue.

Quantel Corporation's Paint Box was the first widely used image-manipulation program for video (commercial television). In the mid-1980s, the IBM Targa board was marketed, a highly versatile, not terribly expensive "frame grabber" and digitizer that could be locked into or mixed with a video signal. Fairly sophisticated programs for the Macintosh computer include Image Studio, Digital Darkroom, and Studio 8. The Amiga's more recently introduced Toaster puts fairly complex animation within the reach of the masses of computer-imaging lovers, or at least those with the patience to learn the program. Video-production programs can now operate through low-end computers and inexpensive software.

29. See "The Rapidly Moving World of Still Imaging," *MPCS Video Times* (New York, Summer, 1988), pp. 28–33. Curiously, this unsigned article, which runs through the various applications of still-video imaging, describes the equipment's uses in law enforcement, saying that it can survey scenes "so that the videotape or stills pulled from it can be used as demonstrative evidence which can hold up as proof in a court of law" (p. 30). Of course, the equipment is also used for surveillance by police and by employers seeking evidence of employee theft. There is no suggestion in the article that these images *can be* manipulated and falsified, making them, one would think, essentially useless as courtroom evidence. Recall the instinctive response of the Califomia state trooper described above. As the case of Rodney King has demonstrated, the use of amateur or "home video"—in which the operator is privileged over the user itself increasingly figures in law and public discourse. 30. *Ibid., p.* 30, and Carol G. Carlson, "Medical Imaging," in Rutgers University's *Matrix* (Spring, 1986), pp. 10–12.

31. Hans Kuhlmann, general manager of marketing and sales, consumer and professional division, Agfa Corporation, speaking on the topic "Productivity—Preparing for the Future," at the Association of Professional Color Labs twenty-first annual convention in Hawai in 1988. Quoted in the convention report in *Photographic Processing* (March, 1989), p. 36.

32. W. Richard Reynolds, "Computers Take Animation Beyond Cartoons: Lifelike Images May Rival Actors," Dallas *Morning News* (March 28, 1988), Sec. C., pp.1–2. Reynolds could not have actually seen the Thalmanns' efforts. For the sake of accuracy, despite the *Morning News* (which misspells the Thalmanns' name), *Rendez-vous d Montreal is* generally credited primarily to Nadia Magnenat-Thalmann, who is currently professor of communication and computer science at the University of Genf in Switzerland (Daniel Thalmann now teaches in Geneva), and her—or their—computer lab, Miralab. *Rendezvous*—which is in English—combines Sleeping Beauty with Pygmalion; the male prince calls up and animates the lovely but reluctant female.

33. All quotations from Reynolds, op. cit., p. 2.

34. Jean Baudrillard, "Requiem for the Media," in *For a Critique of the Political Economy of the Sign* (New York: Telos Press, 1981), p. 172. Italics in original.

35. Collectively known as CAD, for computer-aided design, and CAD/CAM, computer-aided design [and] computer-aided manufacturing. Although the present article focuses on graphics and office work using video terminals, computer technology and its ability to monitor and control workers applies to industrial workers just as well. The reorganization of work in order to increase managerial control has been a major focus of labor studies. See, for example, Richard Edwards, *Contested Terrain: The Transformation of the Workplace*

in the Twentieth Century (New York: Basic Books, 1979), for a broad discussion of the changed nature of work. Some unions, such as the Newspaper Guild and the Communication Workers of America, have gotten some restrictions on computer monitoring written into their contracts, and some industrial unions have gained some say in automated processes. See Andrew Zimbalist, "Worker Control over Technology," *The Nation* (Nov. 17, 1979), pp. 488–489; and a trio of articles—David Moberg, "The Computer Factory and the Robot Worker," Harley Shaiken, "The Brave New World of Work in Auto," and "The Great Computer Heist of Jobs, Skill and Power," an interview with representatives of U.S. auto unions—all in *In These Times* (Sep. 19–25, 1979), pp. 11–14. See also notes 50 and 51.

In an art-related field, computers and lasers are used to produce sophisticated copies of very expensive period furniture. These copies—warps, fades, and all—revive the market for upmarket fakes, but now it seems unnecessary to pretend that the copies are authentic antiques in order to command very high prices.

36. See, for example, "Keystroke Cops," *Dollars & Sense,* No. 118 (July/Aug., 1986), p. 15. The paranoic term "surveillance," as opposed to the more neutral "monitoring," accurately conveys the perception of those so monitored that they are in a situation not unlike covert war.

37. According to the *Village Voice* (Katherine Silberger, "The Electronic Snitch" [Sep. 18, 1990], p. 83), about 85 percent of monitored workers are women. The article quotes a 1989 ad for Close-up LAN, a networking program tying computer "work stations" together: "Look in on Sue's computer screen. You monitor her for awhile . . . in fact, Sue doesn't even know you're there!"

38. The union's full name is "9 to 5, the National Association of Working Women." In 1986, 9 to 5 issued a report entitled *Compuler Monitoring and Other Dirty Tricks* (Cleveland, Ohio). It reported, among other findings, that monitored workers lost much more work time to illness than unmonitored workers did.

In 1980 the National Institute of Occupational Safety and Health (NIOSH) reported a study of computer-monitored clerical workers at Blue Cross/Blue Shield (the nation's largest private medical insurer) showing that they suffered increased rates of "depression, anxiety, instability, fatigue, and anger" ("Keystroke *Cops," op. cit.*).

In 1985 Quebec filmmaker Sophie Bissonnette produced a four-part film entitled *Quel Numéro—What Number?* about women working as telephone operators, grocery check-out clerks, secretaries, and mail sorters. Also in 1985, Britain's Granada Television produced "Terminal: VDTs and Women's Health," and Judy Jackson produced "Hired Hands," about women secretaries, for that country's Channel 4. Questions about VDT use by women inevitably come around to the effects of electromagnetic radiation on reproductive health; see also notes 42 and 49.

39. See Diana Hembree and Sarah Henry, "A Newsroom Hazard Called RSI," *Columbia Journalism Review,* Vol. 25, No. 5 (Jan/Feb 1987), pp. 19–24, which also mentions the stressful role of computer surveillance.

40. Concern over RSI has spread, despite its underplaying in the news (see note 51). In i'Hand Injuries in Workplace Ignite Battle" (*New York Times,* June 3, 1992, p. Bl), reporter Donatella Lorch referred to repetitive stress injuries as "one of the fastest growing workplace disabilities" and describes an attempt to consolidate a number of lawsuits over the issue. (Many manufacturers of this injury-inducing equipment are being sued.) But why didn't the *Times* refer to RSI in the headline? (See also Barnaby J. Feder, "As Hand Injuries Mount, So Do the Lawsuits," *New York Times,* June 8, 1992, p. Dl). Under workmen's compensation rules, injured workers may not sue their employers, but the companies involved include the *Times* and other newspapers, as well as civil-service, telephone, and insurance entities.

41. Paul Brodeur, "The Magnetic Field Menace," *MacWorld* (July, 1990). See also Brodeur's books *The Zapping of America* (about microwave radiation) and *Currents of Death* (about electromagnetic fields) as well as his articles in *The New Yorker,* "Annals of Radiation" (July 9, 1990) and "Department of Amplification" (Nov. 19, 1990). (After *Currents of Death* appeared, an interview with Brodeur was published in *People* magazine on Nov. 27, 1989.) See also Deborah Branscum, "Washington Rethinks ELF Emissions," and Jerry Borrell, "Technology and Science Policy in the Late Twentieth Century: ELF Emissions" (both *MacWorld,* December, 1990). The newsletter *VDT News,* published by Louis Slesin in New York City, monitors computer-related health and safety issues. A "geobiologist" at the Califomia Institute of Technology, Dr. Joseph Kirschvink, has suggested that minuscule crystals of a highly magnetic material, magnetite, that apparently is synthesized by the brain may respond to ELF and may therefore be the reason that such radiation adversely affects the body. (See Sandra Blakeslee, "Magnetic Crystals, Guides for Animals, Found in Humans," *New York Times,* May 12, 1992).

42. Jean Báudrillard, "The Precession of Simulacra," Simulations, New York Semiotext[e], pp. 1-79.

43. Guy Debord, *La Societe du Spectacle* (Paris: Buchet/Chastel 1976); translated as *The Society of the Spectacle* (Detroit: Black & Red, 1970; revised, 1977). The book, which presents a numbered series of propositions—221 of them—is not paginated.

44. Ludwig Feuerbach, *The Essence of Christianity,* 1841; English translation by George Eliot, 1854.

45. John Rockwell, "Photo File of World's Wonders," *New York Times,* March 5, 1992.

46. UNESCO's new director, Federico Mayor, is Spanish, as is La Caixa bank. (I won't comment about Barcelona, the city aiming to be the international cultural capital of the nineties.) Photography, digitization, preservation—this is the new "depoliticized" agenda of an agency that, under its previous (African) director, had attempted to address issues of information control by the developed West, particularly the United States. Its efforts to work toward what it called a New World Information and Communication Order led to a bitter campaign and boycott against it in the West, which labeled its efforts "press censorship." Under Mayor, who is actively seeking U.S. funding and involvement, UNESCO claims to have tumed toward "universality." See also "Unesco Comes Knocking, Seeking U.S. Help," *New York Times,* March 1,1992.

47. Annan, a sort of recordist-photographer, of whom there were many, was working for the Glasgow's improvement trust. Marville, who had previously photographed medieval buildings for the committee on historical monuments, published numerous views of pre-Haussmann Paris. Atget worked for the city of Paris and also compiled archives of views on his own. The Society for Photographing Old London operated in the 1870s and 1880s. The municipal efforts coincided to some degree with tourist-oriented photographic collections.

48. As we learn, for example, from the different 'readings' by different juries of the home videotape of the Rodney King beating in Los Angeles.

49. On transmission devices, see John Durniak's untitled *New York Times* "Camera" column for March 15, 1992, subtitled "A photographer develops a fast transmitting device that makes editors smile." On digitized, compressed video images, see Rachel Powell, "Digitizing TV into Obsolescence," *New York Times* (Oct. 20, 1991). On encryption, see John Markoff, "Experimenting with an Unbreachable Electronic Cipher, *New York Times* (Jan. 12, 1992), which refers to government efforts to impose an encryption standard that industry finds inadequate but does not take up the question why the government objects to the other, more reliably secure and efficient, standards.

50. See Stewart Brand, Kevin Kelly, and Jay Kinney, "Digital Retouching: The End of Photography as Evidence of Anything," *Whole Earth Review* (July, 1985), pp. 42–49.

51. And perhaps despite even Debord's own recent changes and revisions.

52. Needless to say, this does not characterize Americans alone; only consider, for another example, the Germans' tumultuous support for the absurd promises of Helmut Kohl's CDU as unification neared in late 1990. During the Gulf War, the responses of the public in both the U.S. and Great Britain to stage-managed news provided another case in point. Although in the latter instance electronic imaging on television and in the newspapers was integral to the war "story," these approaches were different only in kind, not in strategy or effects, from the propaganda efforts in earlier wars.

Glossary

ACR (Achromatic Color Replacement). Also known under the general terms Achromatic Reproduction, ICR, (Integrated Color Removal) and GCR, (Gray Component Replacement) and PCR, (Polychromatic Color Removal). Traditionally, color printing has been based on the concept that it is necessary to print cyan, magenta, and yellow inks, reinforcing the overprinted areas with black to give neutrality and depth of color. In practice the three colors C, M, and Y cannot produce a satisfactory black on their own, and black ink is used only to assist the color inks. ACR is one means of calculating the CMYK proportions of the printed color. It replaces the neutral element of the color with an equivalent proportion of K (black) and adjusts the remaining CMY values to suit. In the extreme, ACR can enable printing with only two colors (selected from C, M, and Y) and black although it is seldom used this way.

Advantages of achromatic reproduction (ACR):

1. Reduced ink consumption and therefore reduced cost.

2. Reduced ink drying times.

3. Faster printing rates.

4. More stable printing conditions.

5. Stable gray balance.

6. Shorter make-ready times.

It is important not to confuse the achromatic process with the very different process UCR (Under Color Removal).

A/D (Analog to digital conversion). When a ball is thrown into the air, the eye perceives its smoothly flowing motion. This analog perception of the world cannot be handled by digital computers—the information must be converted into a series of numbers before it can be processed. In this case the numbers would record perhaps the height of the ball at regular intervals from the time it was thrown. Computers are very good at storing numbers. Later, those numbers make it possible to reconstruct a graph of specific heights at specific times. The accuracy of the graph depends upon how frequently the measurements were made and the resolution of the height information. This process is known as *digitization* or *quantization*. By dividing an image up into small rectangles (pixels) the brightness and colour of each pixel can be measured and turned into numbers (digital values). Conveniently for the computer, a high-quality image can be saved by measuring the Red, Green, and Blue or the complementary Cyan, Magenta, Yellow, and Black components and allowing 256 levels of each. (Computer buffs will recognise that 256 = 8 bits = 1 byte.) The speed of measurement depends upon the method used to scan the image but it can easily reach several million measurements every second.

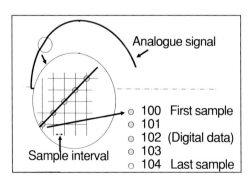

Additive Primaries. Colored lights in red, green, and blue, which when combined with each other in equal proportions produce white. Other colors may be produced by mixing different proportions of each light source. Video monitors use this principle to produce color television images. Input scanner detectors sense red, green, and blue components of the scanned image before electronic conversion to printing colors of cyan, magenta, yellow, and black. Output transparency recorders generate red, green, and blue from input information generally supplied in cyan, magenta, yellow, and black electronically recoded to red, green and blue.

Airbrush. A graphic arts tool that sprays a paint and air mixture. Because volume and density are infinitely variable, the subtlety of the conventional airbrush is immense. Therefore, a good airbrush is an excellent measure of the quality of an electronic system. A good electronic airbrush is also essential, since without this tool delicate retouching, montaging, and special effects are impossible. Sophisticated design is needed if smooth brush profiles are to be achieved, avoiding coarse splatter effects and closely emulating the subtlety of the conventional airbrush.

Aliasing. Unwanted but predictable components resulting from the combination of signals or inadequate preparation of signals prior to digitization. The signals may be static images, moving images, or even sound. Examples of aliasing are:

(i) In print—moire patterns caused by interference between the printing screen and the image detail, caused by an excess of image information relative to the screening process being used.

(ii) In movie film—the spokes of a wagon wheel rotating in the wrong direction, for example, due to insufficient film frames to reproduce the true motion.

(iii) In television—twinkling of sharp near-horizontal lines due to insufficient scanning lines to reproduce the sharp image.

Aliasing can be avoided by careful hardware and software design. *See* high resolution and anti-aliasing.

Analog. A continuously variable signal. This can be broken down into an infinite number of amplitude levels. In practice, the subdivision is not necessary beyond the natural random variation in the signal—for example film grain, video noise, or microphone hiss.

Analog computer. A device that accepts analog inputs and manipulates them according to some defined function to provide an analog output. Examples can be found in both mechanical (gear boxes, navigational tools) and electronic (signal mixers, scanner color computers, motor speed controls) areas. Although theoretically capable of working with infinite resolution, they are always limited by inherent noise and long-term stability problems. As technology advances, most analog electronic processes at the earliest point in the system chain to avoid these stability problems.

Analog computers formed the basis of the color conversion electronics in early drum scanners.

Anamorphic distortion. The process of changing the perceived shape of an object in an image according to some mathematically defined criteria.

Anti-aliasing. The process of avoiding the effects of **aliasing** by careful system design, usually resulting in the inclusion of image detail filters. These filters can be designed to operate in both horizontal and vertical directions as appropriate and can take many forms.

Archive. The name given to an area used for the long-term storage of information that is not needed from day to day. In electronic terms, archiving may take place onto a high density storage medium (magnetic tape or optical disks for example), which may not have the same speed of access as the working store but does have high data integrity and a long lifetime.

Artifact. An unwanted element or structure created accidentally but usually from a predictable cause. Aliasing is an example of an artifact.

Much effort has been expended to minimize the creation of artifacts in printed images. Input detail filtering can eliminate the effects of digitizing an image, while careful choice of screen angles avoids watermark aberrations (moire fringe) and effects in the halftone image. *See* watermark.

ASCII. Initial letters of American Standard Code for Information Interchange. This is a standard coding system used within the computer industry to convert keyboard input into digital information. It covers all of the printable characters in normal use as well as control characters such as carriage return and line feed. The full table contains 127 elements. Variations and extensions of the basic code are to be found in special applications.

ASIC. ASIC is an acronym for Application Specific Integrated Circuits. ASICs provide a powerful tool for constructing modern computer systems. They are customized designs for specific applications enabling very high packing density and performance relative to standard silicon technology.

Binary. The fundamental construction of information used in digital computers. Binary signals only have two states that have a variety of paired names—for example, on/off, one/zero, high/low, and 0/1. A single binary element is called a **bit**.

Any decimal number in numeric base 10 (0, 1, 2, 3, 4, 5, 6, 7, 8, 9, 10, 11, 12, 13) can be represented in binary by converting it to numeric base 2 (0000, 0001, 0010, 0011, 0100, 0101, 0111, 1000). In numeric base 2, each value may be only a 1 or a 0 (*see* Bit). Each digit in the number is two times the value to its right, with the rightmost value being 1 (8, 4, 2, 1, for example). Thus 6 decimal is 0110 in binary (0+4+2+0). Any mathematical operation in decimal has a parallel operation in binary.

Bit. A single **binary** element, the word bit is derived from the words **B**inary dig**IT**. Bits are usually grouped together in blocks of 8 to make **bytes**. Most computer operations work on byte-sized pieces of information.

Bit pad. This is a two-dimensional surface from which a computer can obtain an accurate co-ordinate of a stylus within its operational area. In simple systems the bit pad may contain a switch activated by pressure of the **stylus** on the pad. In this case the computer can be advised of the XY co-ordinates at which the action is to take place. This simple switch action is not suitable for the sensitive needs of a graphic artist who would need, for example, the Quantel patented process of controlling the density of paint through the pressure applied to the stylus.

Blend. The smooth joining of two colors without leaving any perceptible line at the join. The quality of the blending process in digital painting is a measure of the quality of the system.

Blur. A process applied to digitized images to soften the detail of an image feature. This is analogous to defocusing a camera. In high-quality digital painting systems this effect can be applied selectively to portions of the image—for example it can produce appropriate depth of field in photo-montaged images.

Brightness. A measure of the total amount of light emitted, transmitted, or reflected by an item. Scientifically this is measured in Candela.

Browse.
Browse is a powerful reduced-size multi-image presentation. It enables a user to search for an image using pictures rather than words.

Byte. A collection of 8 bits. These 8-bit sets may represent characters, numerical values, or instructions, according to the application. Each 8-bit byte has 28 values representing 256 distinct possibilities.

In larger systems more than one byte will be used to represent a variable. If two bytes (16 bits) are used there will be 65,536 (216) distinct possibilities. Most computers work in whole bytes or multiple bytes.

Images can be adequately captured, displayed, and manipulated as collections of brightness values each of one byte per primary color. This level of resolution is popular for image scanning, transmission, and storage. It is also on the edge of perception of color change in printed images.

See Dynamic Rounding.

Camera (electronic). A system consisting of lenses and a two-dimensional detector to enable the conversion of images into electronic data.

The detector is typically a choice between **CCD** array and vacuum tube technologies. Both types have specific advantages in certain applications. Both types work by converting light into an electrical charge, which can be accomplished either by dumping to charge amplifiers (CCD) or by scanning the charged surface with an electron beam (tube).

Color camera systems are formed in two basic ways. The first uses three independent detectors, one each for red, green, and blue; whilst the second employs one detector and a selectable color filter. The second solution ensures perfect registration as the same tube face is used for all the colors.

CCD (Charge Couple Device). A photon-to-electron charge converter that is usually arranged in single or two dimensional arrays.

The single dimension array is often found in flatbed scanners where the fixed-pitch array is drawn mechanically over the subject. The limit of resolution is usually the pitch of the individual elements of the array. Two-dimensional arrays are found in cameras. At present they do not possess the spatial resolution or sensitivity of tube cameras.

CCD systems can suffer from individual variations in lowlight and highlight sensitivity from cell to cell. This can cause problems by generating a fixed pattern over the image and it is difficult to compensate for fully.

CEPS. Acronym for Color Electronic Page Setting. *See* DPC.

Choke. The process of reducing the width of linework, generally carried out photomechanically by making repeated contact prints from a positive. The inverse function, Spread, is used to increase the width of linework by using the same process but from the negative image.

Chrominance. The color part of a signal relating to **hue** and **saturation** but not to brightness (**luminance**). Neutral colors (grays) have no chrominance but any color is a combination of luminance and chrominance.

CMYK. Initial letters indicating the printer's primary colors; Cyan, Magenta, Yellow, and (K) black.

Color curves. A mechanism that both permits accurate modification and matching of colors at all stages of the design process and controls color changes within the image. The curves are a set of user-adjustable look-up tables that define a transform to be applied to each primary color, additive or subtractive, in the image.

Color difference. A method of coding color image information. Used in television systems and based on red, green, and blue, the coding works by calculating an equivalent luminance component and subtracting this from each of the color values. Thus, for each point of R, G, B, taken from the color camera, we can calculate:

$$Y \text{ (luminance)} = R+G+B$$
$$R - Y \text{ (red color difference)}$$
$$G - Y \text{ (green color difference)}$$
$$B - Y \text{ (blue color difference)}$$

In broadcast television, this has the advantage of making color images compatible with monochrome (black and white) receiving equipment. The above signals are further encoded before transmission so that they may be reconstructed before viewing.

Color mixing. The complex processes that enable professional electronic systems to mix colors to obtain the same effect they would get from traditional art materials. Compensation should automatically be made for the reduced color gamut available from printing inks.

Color separations. The photographic or electronic result, in positive or negative form, of separating a color image into subtractive color components. A color image will separate into films for cyan, magenta, yellow, and black. The separations are normally produced as dot screen representations.

Composite (comp). A graphic design term for a layout combining elements for image, linework, and text.

Continuous tone. Often shortened to contone, it describes images that contain an apparently infinite range of shades and colors smoothly blended to provide a faithful reproduction of natural images.

Copy. The text element of the page in either formatted or unformatted style.

Copy brush. A means of copying one area of the screen image to another position. This may be achieved using a variety of brush sizes and shapes. It is also known as Clone, Shift, and Texture.

Crisp. A process that operates on the color image to sharpen image detail. It is an electronic equivalent to the scanning process of USM (unsharp masking) except that its implementation in Graphic Paintbox allows selective Crisping by painting with a special brush providing the effect. As with scanner USM, there are several intensities of crisp that may be applied.

Cromalin. An off-press color proofing system that uses separations to construct an image through the successive exposure and application of adhesive polymer-dry powder toners. Manufactured and marketed by Du Pont.

Cut/Paste. A function that permits the cutting out, positioning, and pasting down of full-resolution image patches of any size and shape within a system. The speed at which this may be achieved varies considerably from system to system, and slower systems will limit and reduce productivity.

D/A (Digital to analog conversion). The reverse process to Analog to Digital conversion. Here the binary data is converted back to an analog voltage or level proportional to the value of the binary input data. This

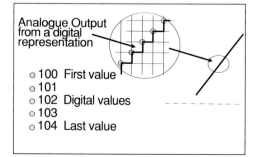

may then be used to control the intensity of a laser recorder or the brightness of output on a television monitor, for example.

Data compression. The amount of data used to represent an image may be reduced if there is much repetition of the data—for example, if there are perfectly uniform areas of color. Many techniques of data compression are available, generally resulting in little compression with no quality loss, but there may be some degradation if much data reduction is demanded.

DDES. Initial letters of the phrase Digital Data Exchange Standard, it is a standard defined by graphics equipment manufacturers to enable image data to be transported between systems without the need to convert to the manufacturers' own coding systems. It is actively supported by major manufacturers including Quantel.

Decoder. A piece of equipment or software that is able to accept data in one format and output it in another.

DECNET. A proprietary system from Digital Equipment Corporation Inc. for networking computer systems and peripherals.

Degradee. The French term for fade. *See* Vignette.

Desk top publishing (DTP). A generic title given to the use of personal computers (PCs) for typesetting, page composition, and image handling. The combination of all these gives total electronic control within a single system over what was traditionally a specialist and segmented operation.

Digitization. The process of converting an analog signal to a digital representation. *See* A/D.

Digitizer. Any system that will take an analog input and convert it into a unique digital representation. Examples include analog to digital converters (A/Ds), bit pads, and mice. Some of these, a mouse and a bit pad, for example, are systems that take a spatial measurement and present it to a computer in a digital form.

Directory. A computer term that describes a means of cataloging the contents of a storage system. Directories may take many forms, including, for example, text descriptions or Browse images.

Disk or Disc (magnetic). A disk coated with magnetic metal oxides upon which magnetic patterns representing image data or text, for example, can be stored. The disk is made to rotate at a constant velocity, either continuously or only when access to it is required.

Modern disk technology enables vast amounts of information to be packed into a small space. A 3.5" diameter removable (floppy) disk can contain more than two million bytes of data, while larger fixed disk types (Winchester) offer over 700 million bytes.

The speed at which data can be passed to and from disks is also important for productivity. Modern technology is able to pass data at a rate faster than 10 million bytes per second.

Dot. A single element in the halftone printing process. The dots, visible through a magnifying lens, vary in size to control the intensity of the printed color.

Each dot is in fact made up of many connected "microdots" generated by the output plotter electronics. The combinations of microdots control both the size and the shape of the finished dot. In a high quality digital prepress system, the information from four pixels will be used to produce a single composite dot. The size of each dot will vary between 0 and 0.08mm (0 and 1/300"), representing 0 to 100 percent density of ink, in a good quality printing job.

Dot Gain. Changes in the halftone dot size that occur as a result of platemaking and printing in the lithographic process. The effect of dot gain is to change the color of the printed material from what was intended as the ink is spread further than the source dot size intended. Corrections for dot gain can be made as the separations are produced, given knowledge of the print process and press settings.

DPC (Digital Page Composing). Also known as EPC or CEPS, this is a system designed to take a range of paper elements (text, linework, and images) and integrate them into a user-specified format.

Image and text inputs to the system may arrive on magnetic tape, by direct system interconnection, or directly from any input scanning system. Output is usually in the form of separations ready for printing via an interface to the output scanner.

DRAM (Dynamic Random Access Memory). A modern computer memory device that offers a very high data-packing density and data rates. Modern devices can store over 1,000,000 bits of information on a 3mm square chip of silicon while consuming less than 1/1000 watt.

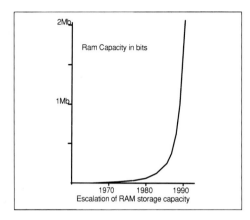

Drop shadow. A graphic arts effect that, by picking a shadow around the edge of two-dimensional shapes gives the impression that the shape is raised above the surface of the paper. This effect is attained because the shadow seems to be cast by a light source positioned above it and offset towards the top or bottom. The sophistication of electronically produced shadow effects depends upon the power of the system.

Drum scanner. A machine for converting a two-dimensional image on a flexible substrate, such as a transparency or printed material into a serial stream of data by fixing the image to a cylinder and rotating the cylinder around its axis. The scanner head illuminates the image as it rotates with a point source of light, forming the first axis of scan, and the transmitted or reflected light is detected by photo multipliers and converted to an electronic signal. The detector and the light source assembly move along the cylinder to form the second axis of the scan.

Most modern scanners provide an output in a digital form through an interface to an EPC system and from there to magnetic tape.

Although the image colors are detected in red, green, and blue, they are converted inside the scanner to cyan, magenta, yellow, and black according to ACR, GCR, or UCR requirements.

Resolution in space is controlled by the digitization rate for the first axis of scan and speed of movement along the cylinder in the second axis, both relative to rotational speed. Effectively, the reading head

describes a spiral along the cylinder. The term is often used for a recorder since earlier scanners included an integrated recorder.

Dynamic Rounding. Eight-bit data is popular for image data exchange and archiving, and it is adequate for most print applications. High-quality graphics computers can operate to a higher precision, which can be carried over to the 8-bit level using dynamic rounding. This Quantel technique is particularly useful for helping to produce smooth vignettes.

Emboss. An effect traditionally produced photomechanically, embossing, can be achieved using certain electronic systems. Electronic embossing, which can take only seconds, can replace complex photographic/mechanical processes that take many hours to complete.

Encoder. A mechanism for converting data from one format to another—for example from RGB to YMCK.

EPC. Initial letters of the term Electronic Page Composition. *See* DPC.

EPIC. A peripheral to Graphic Paintbox, EPIC is an acronym for Electronic Photographic Input Camera. It is a high-definition single-tube camera producing a 1000 line resolution system that can be used as 35mm camera equivalents for applications such as catalogue work. This removes the need for processing and scanning standard photographic material.

Ethernet. A networking system that allows high-speed transfer of data between computer systems and peripherals over a coaxial link.

Flat bed scanner. A useful means of inputting images from flat artwork that does not need the sophistication of a drum scanner or cannot be fitted onto a drum scanner. Modern flat bed scanners use CCD linear array detectors mechanically scanned over the artwork to produce a two-dimensional image. The ultimate resolution is determined by the pitch of the CCD array, typically 12 lpm (300 lpi). Flatbed scanners are usually digitally interfaced directly to systems such as Graphic Paintbox as a fast method for inputting flat artwork, artworks, and roughs.

Floppy disk. A removable magnetic storage medium. Floppy disks come in a range of sizes, including 8 inch, 5.25 inch, and 3.5 inch. The most modern type, 3.5

inch, has more than five times the storage capacity of the older 8 inch variety.

Framestore. A framestore is a two-dimensional array of memory elements used to hold visual information. Modern high-density storage devices permit the construction of framestores with very high resolutions. In the case of Graphic Paintbox XL, the framestore matrix is in excess of 5400 x 3700 elements. Each element in the framestore is known as a pixel.

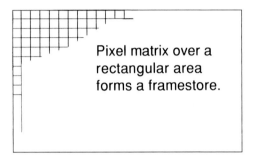

Pixel matrix over a rectangular area forms a framestore.

Gamma. A measure of contrast in photographic processing or, mathematically, the logarithmic relationship between input and output. Straight through (1:1) relationships have a gamma of 1.0, as, for example, a perfect mirror will reflect all light exactly. Color transparency film has a gamma of approximately 2.0 in its relationship between light input and optical density.

GCR (Gray component replacement). *See* Achromatic Separations.

Generation loss. In analog systems, a direct photographic duplicate copy will not be of the same quality as the original. For example, a reproduced photographic transparency will be of lower quality than the original. The loss of quality is referred to as generation loss.

Digital data does not suffer from generation loss when data is copied without processing. *See* Data Compression.

Geometric Shapes. Shapes in two or three dimensions that have a precise mathematical form.

Graduated. Moving smoothly from one state to another. In graphic arts this can be applied to the process of changing smoothly from one color to another over a defined distance. *See* Vignette.

Grain. In film terms, grain is the term used to describe the textured effect of individual crystals of silver on the appearance of the image.

Gravure. A printing process in which recesses on a cylinder are filled with ink and the surplus removed with a blade. The depth of the recess controls the amount of ink trapped and hence the density of any particular cell. Each cell has an equal surface area. The paper contacts the cylinder and lifts the ink from the recesses. Gravure is used for long-run print work such as magazines, journals, and catalogs.

Greeking. A method of simulating the effect of text and typefaces on a page, achieved by filling the selected area with nonsense words based losely on Latin. As these have no distracting meaning in modern use, they enable the balance of a page to be readily judged.

Grid. A regularly spaced set of lines in two dimensions that is used to form a series of positional references. In electronic systems a grid may be used to position text and image information accurately for on-screen page layout and presentation.

Halftone. A printing process in which color intensity is controlled by the size of a discrete dot regularly spaced over the page. The smaller the dot the lower the intensity as the ratio of ink to substrate will be smaller. General printing work is carried out at between 75 and 300 dpi (dots per inch). The tighter the dot packing then the less perceptible they are to the eye and the higher the apparent resolution.

Hard disks. A fixed magnetic storage medium in which the data holding element cannot be removed. Hard disks have very large storage capacity—currently they are up to 1000 Mb—and because of the way they work, they enable data to be rapidly accessed and manipulated.

Hardware. The physical elements that make up an electronic system.

HDTV (High Definition TV). The next generation of television systems, which permit the display of much more information on the television screen.

BTA in Japan has proposed a standard based on 1125 lines at 60Hz field rate 2:1 interlace. Much equipment is available to support this standard. The Quantel Graphic Paintbox uses this standard for display purposes. Europe has proposed an alternative standard of 1250 lines 50Hz.

An HDTV image would give adequate print quality up to a size of between 3–6 inch (75–150mm). The restriction in size is due mainly to the encoding system which offers only half the color resolution that otherwise might have been expected.

Hue. The color-defining component of a point in an image. Hue combined with saturation fully defines a given color.

ICR. Initial letters of the phrase Integrated Color Removal. *See* ACR.

IEEE-488. A hardware interface designed for medium-speed information transfer between computers and peripherals over relatively short distances.

Ink. The colored liquids used in the printing process. The colors of the inks are usually cyan, magenta, yellow, and black. These colors are defined by international standard. In some cases special colors may also be printed. This usually happens where a solid color of a particular hue or saturation is required without the use of the halftone process.

Interface. A general term used to describe the method by which two independent systems may communicate with each other. The term interface is usually used in reference to electronic system interconnection, but may also refer to the way in which users relate to the equipment they operate.

Interpolation. A mathematical procedure for predicting extra values in a sequence of numbers. This enables smooth transitions between the original numbers in the sequence to occur.

One application of interpolation can be found in considering what needs to be done if we magnify a digital image by a factor of two.

The simple approach would be to double the dimensions of each picture point—after all, there is no further information available. However, the result would be as poor, because the enlarged pixels may be obvious to the eye.

A better solution is to start with the original data and recalculate new data values to fit in the spaces caused by the magnification. This calculated data will more closely fit the original image and it will result in a more pleasant effect. Simpler systems use the values from four existing data points to calculate the new values. This minimizes computer effort, and therefore time, but it does not produce a totally pleasing result. Larger and more powerful systems take the values from the surrounding sixteen data points to more accurately calculate the intermediate values. In practice, this approach is only viable in a hardware implementation—software would be too slow. Interpolation is always necessary whenever images are resized or rotated if quality loss is to be minimized.

Laser. Acronym for Light Amplification by Stimulated Emission of Radiation, Lasers are produced from a source of extremely stable and coherent light, that is pure and of a single color. The small spot size achievable using lasers makes them ideal for scanners and recorders.

Library. An organized collection of items. The library functions of Graphic Paintbox permit rapid search and location of pictures, cutouts, stencils, and palettes either by title or by "browse," the reduced size multi-image presentation also known as thumbnails.

Linear. A relationship between an input and its output where they are connected by a first order mathematical expression; that is, a straight line.

The term "linear" is often used as a qualitative term to describe a system where the output matches the input with no distortion.

Linework. Linework is the general term given to areas printed with solid color and thus possessing hard, sharp edges. Examples of this can be found in text, border lines, and boxes.

Linework requires much higher resolution and accuracy of registration than does continuous or half-tone imaging. Because of this, the data volume is potentially very high for a full page. However, because the nature of a line is that it is either present or not present, there is the possibility of encoding the information by run-length-coding to greatly reduce the data volume.

Lithography. Commonly shortened to litho. The word lithography comes from the Greek for "stone writing." The process is an adaptation of the technique of drawing with a grease crayon on stone, with the stone sponged with a special water-based solution and ink. The grease image holds the ink, while the wet stone is protected. Paper is placed on the stone, pressure is applied, and the image is transferred to the paper.

The modern equivalent is a process of reproducing variations in color intensity by controlling the size of the ink spot placed on a page.

This is achieved by a planographic (flat surface)

process in which the ink is applied selectively to the plate by chemically treating image areas to accept ink and nonimage areas to accept water. Inks, being oil based, will not mix with the water. Thus, on a white paper, the larger the spot of ink at each point of the grid (mesh), the denser the color that will appear.

Typical grid (mesh) spacings range from 75 lines per inch (lpi) to 600 lpi or more. Most good-quality work is printed at 300 lpi. This equates to a screen ruling of 150.

By mixing together ink dots of varying size and colors (CMYK) the full range of printable colors can be achieved.

Luminance. The brightness component of a color independent of the color. A black and white (monochrome) photograph is a map of the luminance of the scene as viewed by the film.

It is possible to display luminance without chrominance (color component) but it is not possible to display color without luminance.

LUT (Look Up Table). A digital processing method that takes an input value at one end and outputs another value, a value that need have no specific mathematical relation to the input.

An LUT can be made to perform many tasks. For example, it can add or subtract a constant from the input or multiply or divide the input values. As well as performing these linear transformations, the LUT provides a convenient method of distorting the input signal in some pre-defined way.

For example, LUTs can be used to provide accurate color conversion and matching processes precisely because of their highly stable and very flexible operation.

Magnify. The process of making the original picture information cover a larger area than it would do naturally without detracting unduly from the picture quality. *See* interpolation.

Mag tape. Magnetic tape is the current industry standard mechanism for transporting the large data files that are produced by prepress systems. Supplied in reels of up to 3600 feet long, these tapes hold digitally stored patterns representing an image—approximately 150,000,000 bytes of information on 2400 feet of tape. Although magnetic tape forms a standard mechanism for carrying the data, the way in which the data is stored on the tape is not standardized. For example, a digitized continuous-tone image in CMYK values may be stored

as pixels placed sequentially CMYKCMYK, or as whole images of C then M then Y, Scanned left to right or top to bottom.

Mask. *See* stencil.

Matrix. A multidimensioned array of data used to compute complex results from inputs of many interacting variables.

The RGB to CMYK conversion requires the use of a three-dimensional matrix to accurately solve any of the transformations.

Metamerism. An effect where two objects with differing spectrophotometric curves appear to be the same color when viewed under some lighting condition but different in color under others.

Micro-floppy. A term used to describe a type of 3.5 inch removable magnetic disk commonly found on modern equipment.

Micro processor. The heart of modern computing systems, it appears as a single integrated circuit supported by many other elements to provide the primary intelligence of a computer.

Minicomputer. A system at whose heart lies a microprocessor or multiple microprocessors to provide a complete computing environment.

Moire pattern. In color printing the term describes an irregular and unwanted conglomeration of screen dots of the different printing inks, which cause disturbing patterns or patches, either over the whole image or in certain color combinations. Moire is caused by incorrect screen-angling.

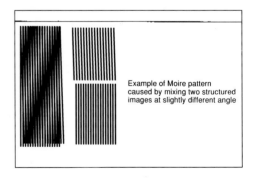

Example of Moire pattern caused by mixing two structured images at slightly different angle

Monochrome. An image printed in a single color, not necessarily black, but covering all the necessary shades to describe the image fully.

Montage. Term used in the graphic industry for a number of operations, including photomontage—a combination and often blending of images

montage (of pages)—page make-up

montage (of pages)—mounting several color separation films of one printing color in register for subsequent transfer to the printing form.

Mouse. A device that controls the movement of the cursor on the screen of a computer terminal. With a Mouse you can call up programs, or menus, activate functions, and determine coordinate-points, as long as your computer can support this type of user-interface.

The mouse has a limited use in painting systems because it has no pressure sensitivity and therefore cannot control color density.

Negative. The inversion of positive. In graphic art, this term is generally applied to images, where the luminance values are inverted (black becomes white and vice versa) and colors are represented by their corresponding complementary color values, for example, red becomes green in a negative).

Negative color film. A film material in which colors are represented by their negative components. It carries a built-in orange-colored mask, which prevents color shifts that otherwise may occur when the image is photographically enlarged from a color negative.

Because of these characteristics (complementary colors, luminance-inversion, and inherent mask) it is practically impossible to produce correct color separations from color negatives unless a negative analyser is used.

Network. Connection between computers and their peripherals that allow every user to access the computer and communicate with other users.

Long Distance Networks (LDN). Bridging cities, countries, and continents, they usually make use of the existing communications facilities of telecom organizations or other privately organized long distance network owners.

Local Area Networks (LAN) are widely used to interconnect computers and peripherals within one site.

See also DECNET and ETHERNET (Trademarks of Digital Equipment Corp).

NTSC (National Television Systems Committee). A broadcast engineering advisory group that produces the standard commonly used for the color television in the U.S., Canada, and Japan.

An NTSC image would give adequate print quality up to a size between 1.5–2.5 inch (32–60mm). The restriction in size is due mainly to the encoding system, which offers only half the color resolution that may otherwise be expected.

Offline. Not connected. For example, a computer printer may be disabled by switching it "Offline." It can also be used when information entered into a computer is processed at a later time, without the operator being present. Many EPC and graphic systems manipulate the actual data after a job has been set up by an operator. The offline component of the job takes much longer than the initial set-up. This may be referred to as "post processing" and forms a major limiting factor to the efficiency of such systems.

Offset. A printing process that uses an intermediate medium to transfer the image from the plate on to the paper. For example, offset litho uses a rubber roller wrapped around a cylinder.

On line. The opposite of offline, it transfers data from one device to another via a direct link. On-line connections require that the linked devices "understand" their data formats and structures and can keep up with the speed of the data transfer.

Optical storage. A form of storing digital data using technology similar to optical audio, or video disks. The advantages to this form of storage include its being extremely compact, allowing rapid access to specific parts of the contents, exposing the write/read system to only a low risk of damage or "head crash."

The main disadvantage is that it is slow at 150–500 KB/sec compared to magnetic disks which run at 1000–20,000 KB/sec.

There are two forms of optical disks:

WORM (Write Once Read Many) Disks: are a permanent store. They cannot be rewritten but they can be read over and over again.

Erasable Disks: These can be used repeatedly. Before rewriting erasable optical disks, the previous contents have to be "erased." (They are not automatically erased during rewriting, as is magnetic storage media.)

Optics. The term used to describe the physical elements of a system in which light is used.

Paintbox. The registered trademark of Quantel's real-time electronic graphic systems.

There are two categories of Paintboxes: the VIDEO Paintbox, which works with picture resolution as required in the video industry; and the GRAPHIC Paintbox, which works with picture resolution as required in the graphics industry (5400 x 3700 pixels equivalent to an A-3 double spread page at a printing screen of 150/inch–60cm).

PAL (Phase Alternating Line). The 625 line 50 Hz composite television system widely used in Europe and many other parts of the world, PAL is derived from the NTSC system but avoids the hue shift caused by electrical distortion in the transmission path.

A PAL image would give adequate print quality up to a size between 1.5–2.5 inch (32–60mm). The restriction in size is due mainly to the encoding system, which offers only half the color resolution that may otherwise be expected.

Paper sizes. There are internationally agreed-upon sizes for paper sheet stock. The ISO system used in most countries is based on three series of sizes—A,B, and C. These base sizes are then subdivided along the longest length to produce the next size down. The proportions of the sheet remains constant by this process of subdivision.

A0 has an area of 1 square meter, permitting direct measurement of paper weight—(grams/sq.m).

Some of the more common varieties for A and B are shown below.

```
A6 : 148mm x 105mm  5.83” x 4.13”
A5 : 210mm x 148mm  8.27” x 5.83”
A4 : 297mm x 210mm  11.69” x 8.27”
A3 : 420mm x 297mm  16.54” x 11.69”
A2 : 594mm x 420mm  23.39” x 16.54”
A1 : 841mm x 594mm  33.11” x 23.39”
A0 :1189mm x 841mm  46.81” x 33.11”
RA6 : 152mm x 107mm 5.98” x 4.21”
RA5 : 215mm x 152mm  8.46” x 5.98”
RA4 : 305mm x 215mm  12.00” x 8.46”
RA3 : 430mm x 305mm  16.93” x 12.00”
RA2 : 610mm x 430mm  24.00” x 16.93”
RA1 : 860mm x 610mm  33.86” x 24.00”
RA0 :1220mm x 860mm  48.00” x 33.86”
SRA6 : 160mm x 112mm  6.30” x  4.41”
SRA5 : 225mm x 160mm  8.86” x  6.30”
SRA4 : 320mm x 225mm  12.60” x  8.86”
SRA3 : 450mm x 320mm  17.72” x 12.60”
SRA2 : 640mm x 450mm  25.20” x 17.72”
SRA1 : 900mm x 640mm  35.43” x 25.20”
SRA0 :1280mm x 900mm  50.39” x 35.43”
B6 : 176mm x 125mm  6.93” x 4.92”
B5 : 250mm x 176mm  9.84” x 6.93”
```

```
B4 : 353mm x 250mm  13.90” x 9.84”
B3 : 500mm x 353mm 19.68” x 13.90”
B2 : 707mm x 500mm 27.83” x 19.68”
B1 :1000mm x 707mm  39.37” x 27.83”
B0 :1414mm x1000mm 55.67” x 39.37”
216.0mm x 279.4mm 8.50” x 11.00”
431.8mm x 558.9mm 17.00” x 22.00”
635.0mm x 965.2mm 25.00” x 38.00”
965.2mm x 1270mm  38.00” x 50.00”
```

Parallel processing. The technique by which all levels of a process are carried out simultaneously. The term also refers to a type of computing hardware, sometimes called an "array processor," that carries out multiple mathematical computations at the same time. The process is very necessary for micro-processor based image manipulation where the processor speed is small compared to the image data sizes and a desirable level of operator speed.

Parallel transfer disks. They contain many read/write heads, all capable of outputting simultaneously (in parallel). This allows data to be transferred to or from the disk at very high speeds (in excess of 10 MB/sec). With careful design, these disks can be used for random-access real-time picture storage.

PCR. Initial letters of the term Polychromatic Color Removal. See ACR.

Peripheral. Originally this was outside border line. In the context of computers systems, it means the additional devices connected to the CPU (Central Processing Unit). Such peripherals include scanners, electronic cameras, disks, mag tape drives, recorders, printers, and so on.

Pixel. Picture Element, a common name given to one sample of digital picture information. It is a shortened version of picture cell, and also known as PEL.

Portability (of data). This refers to the ability to transfer data from one system to another. If this is possible then the data is said to have portability—data on magnetic tapes is portable if it may be read by different systems.

Positive. In the context of an image, a positive image is one that when viewed represents light, shade, and color in the normal sense, and is recognized as such. *See* Negative for description.

Press. In the graphic industry, press is used as an abbreviation of printing press or printing machine. Every printing method requires its specific printing press and shows its special printing characteristic. Even printing presses of the same type have their individual characteristics, identified in their individual "printing curve" which identifies, for example, the machine's dot gain.

Pressure sensitive pen. An electronic pen, which, in conjunction with a digitizing tablet, not only defines the position but also a second parameter, pressure. *See* Stylus.

Proof. A trial printer sheet or copy, made before the production run for the purpose of checking color and content. The proof must allow the prediction of the quality of the real print, ideally making a costly proof-print run unnecessary.

There are many different proofing systems in use: the Cromalin (Du Pont) and Matchprint (3M) are the most widely used today.

Great efforts are being made by a number of manufacturers to launch a digital proofing system, which will produce a qualified proof directly from a digital image data source. *See* Thermal Proofer.

Quantization. *See* Digitization.

QWERTY. Standard British·or American typewriter keyboard layout, so-called because it is the word formed by the first six letters on the keyboard.

Random noise. Random variation in analog signal level where no information is present. In audio terms this manifests itself as hiss or white noise. Pure digitally generated signals have no random noise, which can cause problems under certain circumstances—for example, in electronically generated vignettes. Film grain may be regarded as random noise. *See* Dynamic rounding.

Raster. A regular progressive scanning of a two-dimensional area.

In the graphic industry, the dissolution of a continuous tone image into a multitude of dots that vary in size but are placed at an identical distance from one another. By varying the size of the dots it is possible to modulate the amount of printing ink (usually Y, M, C, or K) discharged onto the substrate.

If a coarse raster is used (for low quality paper) the dots may be visible with the bare eye.

If extremely fine rasters are used, the number of discernible tonal values decreases, especially in any of the shadow areas.

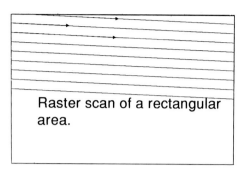

Raster scan of a rectangular area.

Raster (scan). A raster image is one in which each individual picture element is represented by a numerical value indicating intensity.

A raster scan is a progressive reading of an image, usually starting at the top left corner and moving toward the top right. After this first line, subsequent raster scans are made adjacent to the first scan until the whole image is covered.

Registration. The exact positioning of the four separation films or four printing colors on top of each other consecutively.

The human eye, even unaided, is quite sensitive to misregister, which is clearly seen as color borders that spread out from a contour in the image.

Resolution. Resolution controls the degree to which we may perceive changes in color or physical spacing. A low-resolution system may exhibit coarse color steps or large visible areas of solid color. Digital systems must be carefully designed to prevent either of these effects. There is a finite limit to the need for ever-increasing resolution as there is no point in resolving beyond the perception of the human eye under normal viewing conditions. Digital systems in print must at least equal these requirements.

Retouching. The changing of the amount of value of color in a part of an image. Retouching principally serves two purposes; a) to add or delete elements to/from the picture, and b) to adapt color separations to the printing conditions.

RGB. The abbreviation of red, green, and blue, the additive primary colors (as opposed to Y, M, C, the subtractive colors).

RIP. Acronym for Raster Image Processor. PC-based graphic workstations usually produce files in a very compact form, based on vector definitions. However, these are not directly suitable for output as all plotters and scanning systems need raster data to operate. RIP technology provides the link between vector and raster systems. Postscript (™ Adobe) is an example of a vector data generator. *See* Vector and Raster.

Rotate. To turn something (for example a picture or a cutout) around its axis. In image processing this is a very computer-intensive process because the position of every single pixel has to be recalculated and additional pixels must be generated.

Run Length Coding. A system of encoding for digital data to reduce the amount of storage needed to hold the data without loss of information. Each coded item consists of a data value and the number of adjacent pixels with that data value. This is a very efficient way of encoding large areas of flat color as used in linework and text. *See* Data Compression.

Sampling. Process applied to convert an analog signal into a series of digital values. *See* A/D.

Saturation. The amount of a primary color applied on any specific area as a percentage of the maximum.

Scaling. Changing the size of an image or a cut out—that is, changing its dimensions in both the X and the Y directions. Sometimes known as "Dispro," a shortened version of disproportionate. *See* Interpolation.

Screen Angles. The degree of rotation under which each screen dot of a print color or separation is positioned relative to another print color or separation.

The normal screen-angling is in steps of 15 degrees; for example, (0, +15, +30, +45, or 0, +30, +45, +60) So called "rational" screen angles, which step in 18.4 degrees, are often found in laser typesetters. These screen angles create moire, which can become quite annoying in certain color combinations.

SCSI interface. Initial letters of the phrase Small Computer Systems Interface. A parallel data transfer mechanism widely used within computer systems for data communications over short distances, it is often pronounced "Scuzzi."

Separation. Term used in the reprographic industry to describe the films, which represent the yellow, magenta, cyan, and black content of an image. By printing these four "separations" one on top of the other, most of the mixed colors of the image can be generated in the printing process.

Serial communications. A computer communication system where data elements follow one after the other. Commonly used to describe a single wire interface used for low-speed applications between computers and peripheral devices.

Serial processing. The description of any process in computing and printing that consists of a number of discrete stages carried out sequentially. This is the method in which traditional photographic reproduction was carried out. Serial processing, resulting in generation loss, is the reason for a certain loss in quality of the end result. Digital processing avoids such losses.

Shade. A function that allows the luminance (brightness) of an image to be either increased or decreased. It is more valuable in systems that permit this to happen selectively.

Shadow. The information contained in the lowlight—darker—areas of an image.

Shift. Another term to describe copy, shift refers to the physical shift distance between the source image and the destination point within the image. It allows one part of the image to be transferred to another. It is a useful retouching tool for copying texture, and it is especially good for extending backgrounds and removing scratches.

Silk screen. A print method where a fine mesh screen tightly drawn across a frame is selectively protected by a film. The printing ink is forced through the unprotected areas by a blade (squeegee) onto the substrate. Because of the relatively coarse mesh that is used, resolution and density range are limited. The method does have the advantage of being able to print onto a variety of substrates ranging from car windows to microwave ovens using a wide variety of inks.

Smear. The process readily achievable within the digital domain whereby an image can be manipulated as if the ink or paint were still wet. Useful to create "speed" effects or to show flow from bottles or indeed as an artistic or creative effect.

Smooth. Another name for Blur. A defocusing effect.

Software. The instruction set, or program, running on or in a computer, it tells the hardware what, when, and how to function.

Many electronic painting systems are software based, as they use a proprietary computer and complex software to perform image data manipulations. This is time-consuming and means the system becomes ponderous to use.

The optimum approach uses specifically designed and built hardware that will only require "housekeeping" instructions from the software. Thus operational instructions and manipulations are carried out in realtime—the creative process is not compromised.

Solarization. An effect whereby subtle changes of colors are replaced by continuous tones or even different colors altogether, it is achieved by reducing the number of available colors from the typical 16 million down to between 10 to 100 in discrete steps.

Solid state. A term describing the nature of the electronics since the thermionic valve was displaced by the transistor. In the 1950s, electronics was dominated by the valve, a device that used a vacuum-filled glass tube in which electrons flowed. The transistor uses a solid semiconductor material known as silicon as the active medium—hence the term solid state.

Spatial resolution. The smallest feature of an image that can be detected as a fraction of the total image. For example, 5400 picture points will represent 5.4 inches at 1000 lpi, giving a spatial resolution capability of 1/1000th of an inch. However, at 150 screen (300 lpi) this would represent 18.13 inches. It is a measure of the ultimate sharpness of an image.

Spread. The process, generally carried out photomechanically by making repeated contact prints from a negative, of enlarging the width of linework. The inverse function, Choke, is used to reduce the width of linework by using the same process but from the positive image. Spread is done to ensure that there is no gap between the linework and the surrounding area. The linework, now much larger, spreads over from its original area to give an overlay, simplifies the printing process by reducing the need for absolute accuracy of the press. *See* Choke.

Stencil. A term used in the reprographic industry to describe an overlay that forms a protective layer over a portion of an image to isolate it from the whole. Conventionally a stencil would be produced manually or photographically. In electronic systems, the ease of creation and modification of stencils is a measure of their quality and power. Where available, the ability to cut out complex and soft-edged shapes through a stencil can form an important benefit in the system usage. In better systems, masks can be readily produced, either by using any of the brush styles or automatically, using set luminance and chrominance parameters.

Stylus. An alternative to the mouse as a control system for electronic devices. Its resemblance to a pen or brush makes for greater operator familiarity and can offer significant benefits over a mouse, such as pressure sensitive operation.

Subtractive. Colored pigments (paint or ink), cyan, magenta and yellow, that when combined with each other in equal proportions produce black (but only in an ideal world). These colors are known as subtractive primaries—printing processes are based on them.

Supercomputer. A loose term meaning a computer whose speed (measured in instructions per second) exceeds a nominal 100 million instructions per second (MIPS). A typical office personal computer is rated at about 1 or 2 MIPS. A Norsk Data or Cray Supercomputer is rated at about 200–300 MIPS. In comparison, the specifically designed hardware in Graphic Paintbox enables it to work at the equivalent of 1,000 MIPS. This power eliminates post processing, enabling the system to function in real time.

Tablet. A name sometimes used to describe the bit-pad which, in conjunction with the stylus, is used to control certain graphic production systems. The tablet senses the position of the artist's stylus and conveys that information to the control system.

Texture. An impression of surface detail in a two-dimensional image.

Thermal printer/proofer. A device that (usually) connects directly and digitally to a graphics system and outputs an image using a thermal process.

The thermal process is dye sublimation, whereby a linear thermal head, made up of a series of semiconductor elements, is fed with digital information from the graphics system.

Colored films, one each of C,M,Y, and K, are sandwiched between the head and a sheet of receiver paper, which is resin or polymer coated. The heat from the head causes the dye within the film to vaporize or sublimate. This vapor is then deposited onto the paper. The paper and film are moved over the thermal head. The next film color is moved into position and the process is repeated. Note that the proof is con-tone and not screened.

Three-color devices are also available. However, C,M,Y, and K systems provide a more accurate representation of the final printed result.

Tint. A solid color reduced in shade by screening. Tint is specified as a percentage screen of the color. Being a mathematically precise function it may readily be implemented in hardware-based electronic systems. It is not usually practical in software-based systems because of the processing time required. The advantage of electronic tint production lies in the ability to alter existing hues without affecting the gray component of the color. Shadows and highlights are unaffected because they have no hue. In the most powerful systems, the subtlety of application is such that sophisticated photographic retouching may be undertaken.

Transparency. i) The degree of visibility through a solid medium. ii) A sheet of film upon which resides a positive, con-tone image. This sheet of film and image can be a variety of different sizes depending upon the use. A transparency containing an image can of course be rescanned to a different size and as such is an international image transfer medium.

The transparency may be created directly in a camera, in which case it is known as an original and has, if produced correctly, a density range of 3.0.

Transparencies may also be created as copies of the original. Density range suffers in this case.

Electronic graphics systems may create transparencies via transparency units such as MDA™ (MacDonald Detweiler), CLP-300™ (DiNippon), LTV™ (Kodak) or Solataire™ (Management Graphics, Inc.) plus others. In order to create perfect transparencies resolutions up to and beyond 1000 lpi are used. High quantities of image data are therefore necessary. Density ranges of 3.0 are achievable. Transparencies thus created are known as "Second Originals" or "Digital Originals."

Truncation. Truncation is the deliberate limiting of the resolution of a number.

TTL (Transistor Transistor Logic). A generic name given to an early class of logic devices used in electronics and computing. The name derives from the use of two transistors at the output (totem pole). Now superseded by CMOS and ECL logic families, among others, and by ASICs (Application Specific Integrated Circuits) in the very latest designs.

Typography. The name describing all aspects of text production. This highly creative area, traditionally based on photographic processes, has benefited considerably from major advances in electronic production. The fact that digitized text is commonly used at resolutions up to 3000 lpi has proved a major obstacle to the integration of text and color images. The only effective way of using high resolution is to create a system where text and color work are handled by separate dedicated processors within a single control environment.

UCA (Under Color Addition). The inverse function of UCR, UCA is applied in conjunction with GCR because 100% GCR does not produce a good saturated black in the print. Therefore, it is necessary to add a controlled amount of "under color" to the GCR in the black areas. The UCA computation is usually carried out in the scanner.

UCR (Under Color Removal). This is a technique whereby the three-color gray component, where it occurs in shadow and lowlight areas, is replaced with black in the color separations. This replaces the amount of expensive CMY ink with inexpensive black ink. It reduces the amount of ink necessary to reproduce greys with an increase in printing speeds and decreased drying time. Not to be confused with GCR, which affects all three color mixes.

Standard: Y 88%, M 88%, C 95%, K 75%
With UCR: Y 68%, M 68%, C 75%, K 95%

Note that this has only affected the grays, not the colors. It results in a heavier black separation and thinner YMC separations. Modern scanners include the ability to control the neutral (gray) density at which this process starts to take place.

Unsharp masking (USM). Unsharp masking is the name given to the technique with which edges within an image are given a boost in the form of a light or dark line along the transition. This has the effect of giving the image more attack or bite. It can be applied either during scanning or photographically. *See* Crisp.

Vector. Vector is the general term given to a class of graphic drawing systems. Within such a graphic system, a vector is a line specified as a color, and start and end points. This means that a very long line can be stored as the same amount of data as a very short line, since only the size of the numbers change—not the number of numbers. An image would be made up of a large number of these vectors. This can be a very space-efficient way of storing image data but its disadvantages are that it is difficult to manipulate the data mathematically and it is not an easy task to reproduce real data (such as a photograph) purely in terms of vector information.

Vectors are therefore generally constrained to the production of linework, typography, and tints.

Vignette. Another name for a gradation (or graduation) of degradee. This is a transition of color from one particular value of hue and saturation to another over a given distance in a given area. This may happen in the vertical, horizontal, or circular directions.

In electronic systems, vignettes present particular problems if patterning (banding) is to be avoided. Dynamic rounding is a method that effectively eliminates this problem. *See* Dynamic rounding.

Wash. This is a technique whereby the color (both the hue and saturation) of the picture is replaced by another color. It is similar to tint, but affects the saturation as well as the hue.

Web. The printing process using a continuous roll of paper as opposed to single sheets. Web is a faster printing process than sheet fed, and so it is suitable for long print runs.

Word. A fundamental instruction unit within a computer. It may consist of one, two, or four bytes, depending upon which type of processor is in use. It may be data, an instruction, or a memory location.

Work station. A powerful desktop computer, usually but not always networked with others. Many times more powerful than a basic PC and more expensive. Used for processor intensive tasks such as CAD, typesetting, or 3-D modeling.

WORM (Write Once Read Many Times). This describes a digital storage medium (usually optical) to which you may send information (say an image). This image is then stored permanently on the disk. It cannot be erased or altered but it can be read back many times. It is useful for archive purposes.

Zits. Unwanted small picture elements.

Zoom. Similar to magnify in its ability to examine the image detail but without the mathematical interpolation. This enables the exact content of each pixel to be examined and modified as required.

Bibliography

Michael Aaland. *Digital Photography*. Random House, 1994

Dawn Ades. *Photomontage*. Pantheon Books, 1976.

Jonathan Alter. "When Photographs Lie." *Newsweek*, 7/30/90, p. 44

China Altman. "Portrait Show to Open in Compton Gallery," *Tech Talk*, MIT Press, 4/87.

Richard Altman. "The Electronic Image," *Darkroom Photography*, 12/87, p. 38.

Clare Ansberry. "Alterations of Photos Raise Host of Legal, Ethical Issues,"The Wall Street Journal, 1/26/89.

Roger Armbrust. "Computer Manipulation of the News," *Computer Pictures*, 1/85, p. 6.

Robin Baker, *Designing the Future*, Thames and Hudson, 1993.

Roland Barthes. *Mythologies*, Hill & Wang, 1972.

Jean Baudrillard. *Simulations,* Semiotext(e), 1983.

Stanley Baxendale. *The First Computer Design Coloring Book*. Harmony, 1979.

Walter Benjamin. *Illuminations*. Jonathan Cape, 1970,

Jonathan Benthall. *Science and Technology in Art Today*. Thames & Hudson, 1972.

Peggy Bentham. *VDU Terminal Sickness: Computer Health Risks and How to Protect Yourself*. Green Print, 1991.

John Berger. *Ways of Seeing*. Penguin, 1972.

Saul Bernstein. *Making Art on your Computer*. Watson Guptill, 1986.

Derek Bishton. "Digital Dialogues," *Ten 8*, Autumn 91,Vol. 2, No. 2.

David Bolter. *Turing's Man: Western Civilization in the Computer Age*. University of North Carolina Press, 1984.

Daniel Boorstein. *The Image: A Guide to Pseudo Events in America*. Harper & Row, 1961.

Jerry Borrell. "Digital Paint Systems." *Computer Graphics World*, 4/82, p. 61.

Howard Bosen. "Photojournalism, Ethics & the Electronic Age." *Studies in Visual Communication*, 6/85 p. 22.

Stewart Brand. "Digital Retouching, the End of Photography as Evidence." *Whole Earth Review*, 7/85, p. 42.

Stewart Brand. *The Media Lab: Inventing the Future at MIT*. Viking Press, 1987.

Norman Breslow. *Basic Digital Photographs*. Focal Press, 1991.

Malcolm W. Browne. "Computer as Accessory to Photo Fakery." *New York Times*, 7/24/91

Christopher Burnett. "Computers and Art in the Age of the World Picture." *Views*, Spring 88, p. 8.

Nancy Burson, Richard Carling, and David Kramplich. *Composites*. Beech Tree Books, 1986.

C. David Chaffee. *The Rewiring of America: The Fiber Optics Revolution*. Academic Press, 1988.

Jeffrey Chester. "Counterfeiting in the News." *Columbia Journalism Review*, 5/88.

Van Deren Coke. *The Painter & the Photograph*, University of New Mexico Press, 1964.

Majorie Costello. "Filmless Camera." *Omni*, 11/87, p. 169.

Bob Cotton. *Hypermedia*. Phaidon, 1993.

Duncan Davies. *The Telling Image: The Changing Balance between Words and Pictures in a Technological Age*. Oxford University Press, 1990.

Bennett Daviss. "Printbox." *Discover*, 7/90 p. 54.

Joseph Deken. *Computer Images*. Stewart, Tabori & Chang, 1983.

Michael Dertouzos. "Building the Information

Marketplace." *Technology Review*, 1/91.

E. J. Dijksterhuis. *The Mechanization of the World Picture*. New York University Press, 1963.

David Douglas. *Art in the Future*. Praeger 1973.

John Durniak. "Some People Take Pictures with Cameras, and Some Now Make Them on Computers." *New York Times*, 1/19/92.

Jef Edwards. "New Technology & New Legal Quagmires." *Exposure*, 21:1, p. 32.

Arielle Emmett. "Computers & Fine Arts." *Computer Graphics World*, 10/88.

Christopher Evans, *The Micro Millenium*. Viking Press, 1979.

Christopher Evans, *The Mighty Micro*. Viking Press, 1984.

Stuart Ewan. *All Consuming Images: The Politics of Style in Contemporary Culture*. Basic Books, 1988.

Elizabeth Ewen. *Channels of Desire*. McGraw-Hill, 1982.

M. Foucault. *Discipline & Punish*. Vintage Books, 1979.

Herbert Franke. *Computer Graphics, Computer Art*. Springer-Verlag, 1985.

John Free. "Filmless Photos." *Popular Science*, 11/87.

Richard Friedhof. *Visualization: The Second Computer Revolution*. Abrams, 1989.

Barbara Garson. *The Electronic Sweatshop: How Computers Are Transforming the Office of the Future into the Factory of the Past*. Simon & Schuster, 1988.

Ellen Gerken. *Click*. North Light Books, 1990.

Patricia Goldstein. "Seeing Beyond Sight." *Photo Design*, 1/88 p. 36.

E. H. Gombrich. *Art & Illusion*. Princeton University Press, 1960.

R. C. Gonzalez. *Digital Image Processing*. Addison-Wesley, 1977.

William B. Green. *Digital Image Processing: A Systems Approach*. Van Nostrand Reinhold, 1989.

Steve Gross. "Computers Create Specialised Photos." *Minneapolis Star & Tribune*, 2/12/ 87, p. 1M.

Andy Grundberg. "*Ask it No Questions: The Camera Can Lie.*" *New York Times*, 8/90.

Rob Haimes. "Graphic Design Technology Matures." *Computer Graphics World*, 2/88, p. 50.

Rebecca Hansen. "Computers & Photography." *Computer Graphics World*, 1/89, p. 53.

Helen Harrison. "Computer Imaging on Display." *New York Times*, 1/3/88.

Philip Hayward, ed. *Culture, Technology and Creativity*. John Libbey, 1991.

M. Heidigger. *The Question Concerning Technology and Other Essays*. Harper & Row, 1977.

Stephen Hill. *The Tragedy of Technology: Human Liberation Versus Domination in the Late Twentieth Century*. Pluto, 1988.

David Hockney. *Hockney on Photography*. Harmony Books, 1988.

Pam Holmes. "Digital Totems." *Artline*, 1/84.

Gerald Holzman. *Beyond Photography*. Prentice Hall, 1988.

Anne H. Hoy. *Fabrications: Staged, Altered, and Appropriated Photographs*. Abeville, 1987.

Robert Hughes. *The Shock of the New*. Alfred A. Knopf, 1981.

Linda Jacobson. *Cyberarts: Exploring Art and Technology*. Miller Freeman, 1992.

Annabel Jankel. *Creative Computer Graphics*. Cambridge University Press, 1984.

Alain Jeubert. "Photos which Falsify History." *Aperture*, Spring 88, p. 110.

Rory Johnston. "Computer Art Horizons." *The London Times*, 15/1/85.

Estelle Jussim. *Visual Communication and the Graphic Arts: Photographic Technology in the Nineteenth Century*. R.R. Bowker, 1983.

M. Ethan Katsh. *The Electronic Media and the Transformation of Law*. Oxford University Press, 1989.

Toshifumi Kawahara. "World Graphic Design Now," *Fine Art*, Vol. 6, Kodansha Dachi-Shuppan Center Publishing, 1989.

Isaac Kerlow, *Computer Graphics for Artists and Designers*. Van Nostrand Reinhold, 1993.

Stewart Kranz. *Science & Technology in the Arts*. Van Nostrand Reinhold, 1974.

Ronald Labuz. *The Computer in Graphic Design*. Van Nostrand Reinhold, 1993.

John Larish. *Electronic Photography*. Tab Books, 1990.

J. D. Lasica. "Pictures Don't Always Tell Truth." *The Boston Globe*, 1/2/1989, p. 29.

Hans Leopoldseder. *Miesterwerke Der Computerkunst*. TMS Verlag, 1988.

M. S. Livingsone. *Art, Illusion and the Visual System*, Scientific American. 258, no. 1, p. 78.

Phil LoPiccolo. "What's Wrong with This Picture?" *Computer Graphics World*, 6/91, p. 6.

John Lowell. *A–Z Guide to Computer Graphics*. McGraw Hill, 1985.

Tom Macmillan. "Telegenic Charismas." *Computer Graphics World*, 11/87.

Gerry Mander. *Four Arguments for the Elimination of Television*, Quill Publishers, 1978.

Marc Mannheimer. "Computer Art & the Work of Jeremy Gardiner." *Art New England*, 12/87.

Joe Matazzoni. "Outputting Fine Color from the

Desktop." *Step by Step Graphics*, 9/92, p.146.

Patrick McDonnel. "Citizen's Search for Print Perfection." *Step by Step Graphics*, 9/88, p. 92.

Marshall McLuhan. *Understanding Media: The Extension of Man.* Routledge and Keegan Paul, 1968.

Douglas Merrit. *T.V.Graphics-from Pencil to Pixel.* Van Nostrand Reinhold, 1987.

Sherry Milner. "Electronic Video Image Processing: Notes Toward a Definition." *Exposure*, 21:1 '83, p. 22.

William J. Mitchell. *The Reconfigured Eye: Visual Truth in the Post Photographic Era.* The MIT Press, Boston, 1992.

Mondo 2000. *A User's Guide to the New Edge*, Harper Collins, 1992.

Chandra Mukerji. *From Graven Images: Patterns of Modern Materialism.* Columbia University Press, 1983.

Donald Norman. *Things That Make Us Smart.* Addison Wesley, 1993.

Bill Nichols. *Ideology and the Image*, Indiana University Press, 1981.

Michael O'Connor. "The Serious Implications of Digital Image Processing." *Print 40*, 1986, p. 51.

Gary Olsen. *Getting Started in Computer Graphics.* North Light Books, 1989.

Vance Packard. *The Hidden Persuaders.* Longmans, 1957.

Andrew Pollack. "Computer Images Stake Out New Territory." *New York Times*, 7/24/91.

Frank Popper, *Artists of the Electronic Age*, Abrams, 1993.

Mark Power. "Electronic Photography." *Washington Post*, 4/25/87.

William Pratt, *Digital Image Processing*, John Wiley & Sons, 1978.

Frank Presbrey. *The History and Development of Advertising.* Greenwood Press, 1961.

Vivien Raynor. "Computer Reigns at Bronx Museum of the Arts." *New York Times*, 10/25/87.

Michael Real. *Mass-Mediated Culture.* Prentice Hall, 1977.

Sheila Reeves. "Digital Retouching: Is There a Place For It in Newspaper Photography." *News Photographer*, 1/87, p. 23.

Wendy Richmond. *Design and Technology.* Van Nostrand Reinhold, 1990.

Alan Ripp. "Whose Image is it Anyway?" *American Photographer*, 6/87, p. 78.

Fred Ritchin. "Photography's New Bag of Tricks." *New York Times Magazine*, 11/4/84, p. 40.

Fred Ritchin. *In Our Own Image.* Aperture, 1990.

Robert Rivlin. *Algorithmic Image.* Microsoft Press, 1986.

Barbara Robertson. "Bridging the Photo Retouching Gap." *Computer Graphics World*, 11/90, p. 52.

Naomi Rosenblum. *The World History of Photography.* Abbeville Press, 1984.

John Ross. *The Complete Printmaker.* Free Press, 1990.

Aaron Scharf. *Art & Photography.* Penguin, 1974.

Michael Schudson. *Advertising, The Uneasy Persuasion.* Basic Books, 1984.

Joan Scot. *Computergraphia.* Golf Publishing Co, 1984.

Brian Reffin Smith. *Soft Computing in Art & Design.* Addison Wesley, 1984.

Sandra Smith. "Putting Computer Design in the Picture." *Electronic Times*, 1/84.

Susan Sontag. *Against Interpretation.* Dell, 1966.

Bruce Sterling, ed. *Mirrorshades—The Cyberpunk Anthology.* Palladin, 1988.

Pat Sweet. "Electra becomes the Muse of a Blank Canvas." *Computing*, 2/84.

Peter Tatiner. "News Photography Goes Electronic." *Photo District News*, 11/86.

John Vince. *The Language of Computer Graphics.* Van Nostrand Reinhold, 1990.

Patrice Wagner. "CG and PrePress Join Forces." *Computer Graphics World*, 3/83, p. 39.

Patrice Wagner. "Digital Portfolio." *Computer Graphics World*, 12/84.

Joseph Weizenbaum. *Computer Power and Human Reason: From Judgement to Calculation.* W.H. Freeman, 1976.

Kelly Wise. "High Tech Portraits on View." *The Boston Globe*, 6/6/87.

Paul Wombell, ed. *PhotoVideo: Photography in the Age of the Computer.* Rivers Oram Press, 1991.

Gene Youngblood. *Expanded Cinema.* E.P Dutton & Co, 1970.

William Zimmer. "High Tech Images on View." *New York Times*, 4/13/86.

Index